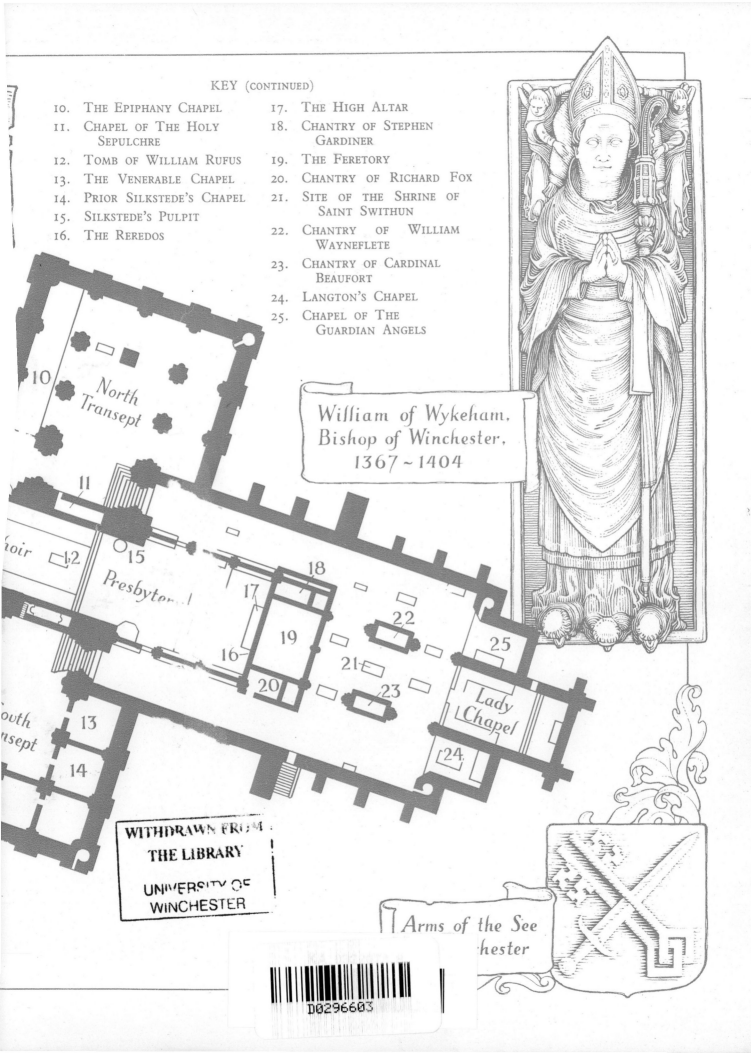

KEY (CONTINUED)

10. THE EPIPHANY CHAPEL
11. CHAPEL OF THE HOLY SEPULCHRE
12. TOMB OF WILLIAM RUFUS
13. THE VENERABLE CHAPEL
14. PRIOR SILKSTEDE'S CHAPEL
15. SILKSTEDE'S PULPIT
16. THE REREDOS

17. THE HIGH ALTAR
18. CHANTRY OF STEPHEN GARDINER
19. THE FERETORY
20. CHANTRY OF RICHARD FOX
21. SITE OF THE SHRINE OF SAINT SWITHUN
22. CHANTRY OF WILLIAM WAYNEFLETE
23. CHANTRY OF CARDINAL BEAUFORT
24. LANGTON'S CHAPEL
25. CHAPEL OF THE GUARDIAN ANGELS

William of Wykeham, Bishop of Winchester, 1367 ~ 1404

North Transept

Presbytery

Choir

South Transept

Lady Chapel

Arms of the See ...chester

THE GLORIES OF
WINCHESTER CATHEDRAL

Winchester Cathedral: the tower and south transept.

THE GLORIES OF
WINCHESTER
CATHEDRAL

By RAYMOND BIRT

Photographs by
A. W. KERR

WINCHESTER PUBLICATIONS LIMITED
16 MADDOX STREET LONDON W.1

First published in mcmxlviii by
Winchester Publications Limited
16 Maddox Street, London, W.1

ACKNOWLEDGEMENT

We wish to acknowledge to Mr. G. E. Bryant, head verger of Winchester Cathedral and for more than twenty-one years a member of its staff, the debts we have accumulated in the preparation of this book. He has been our chief guide to the history of the Cathedral and to its treasures. If we have translated into print and pictures even a small part of his enthusiasm and his love for this ancient place, then the work is good. If we have not then the failure is ours alone. We could not have been more generously or more wisely directed.

We must also acknowledge our obligation to the Dean and Chapter who granted permission for photographs to be taken of the Cathedral.

RAYMOND BIRT
A. W. KERR

MADE AND PRINTED IN GREAT BRITAIN BY L. T. A. ROBINSON, LTD., LONDON, S.W.9

CONTENTS

Part I

THE BUILDING OF THE HOUSE

Part II

THE TREASURES OF THE HOUSE

Part I

THE BUILDING OF THE HOUSE

1 : *The Founders*

I T is astonishing (one says, looking down on Winchester Cathedral from the old Celtic hill fort on St. Catherine's Hill) that the Norman builders should have selected such a site for their great Cathedral. It lies in the heart of the ancient city at almost the lowest part of the Itchen valley. To the south the open fields are silver-veined with streams and drainage ditches. A thousand years ago all this land was a spongy marsh from which springs bubbled and rivulets trickled down to the slow-running River Itchen. Yet on this marsh the Normans chose to build, although at very little distance either to the east or west the ground is firm and dry and offers the builder of a tower some glorious sites from which to dominate the city.

The choice of so undramatic a site, which required the architects to drive mighty piles into soft ground before a single stone could be laid, seems inexplicable—unless perhaps, it was selected because the builders wished to shorten the haul of stone from the barges on the Itchen to the building site.

In fact, the Norman builders had no choice ; or rather, the influence of the magic of place was too powerful for even these ruthless creators of a new order to disregard it. Winchester Cathedral was erected on a marsh because here the Saxons had sanctified the ground with the dust of their kings and the shrines of their saints ; because here the Roman conquerors before them had erected their temples ; and because, before ever the Romans came, the Belgic peoples of the Itchen valley worshipped the fertility of their Mother Earth where the springs most abundantly rose and among which they buried the ashes of their dead.

We can set no term to the years during which the site of Winchester Cathedral was held sacred by our forefathers. All we know is that there has been a continuity of worship here which stretches far beyond the limits of our recorded history. Even when, in the year 635, Saint Birinus landed in Britain with a commission from the Pope to convert the barbarian Saxon chieftains of this island, the sense of the sacredness of the site had survived the terrible years of darkness and slaughter that followed the withdrawal of the Roman legions. From the Saxon king Cynegils, Birinus obtained permission to build a Christian church, and to support the foundation was given a grant of land which extended for seven miles around the city. On Christmas Day 648, with dazzling ceremony, Saint Birinus dedicated Winchester's first Christian cathedral to the worship of God in the names of Saints Peter and Paul. To this day the arms of Winchester Cathedral bear the keys and sword of the two saints to whom the earliest Saxon Cathedral was dedicated. To this day also the bones of Cynegils, first Christian king of Wessex, lie in one of the mortuary chests which stand on the screens of the Cathedral's presbytery.

For hundreds of years after the foundation of the Cathedral, Winchester was the capital of England—the seat of government, the home of the kings, and their resting place when they came to die. Twenty kings were buried in Winchester, and thirty-five made it their capital. Until the time of the Reformation, Winchester was not only the richest see in England, but also provided the English kings, century after century, with their ablest administrators. Few of the long line of Winchester's bishops did not hold one of the high State offices, and all of them were men of great consequence in Church or State. When Edward III established the Order of the Garter in 1346, the Bishop of Winchester was appointed Chancellor of this chivalrous company. The appointment has passed to his successors ever since.

There is nothing left to us now of the old Saxon cathedral, nor of its more splendid successor—a wonder in its day—which was built in the middle of the tenth century by the Benedictine monks of the Priory of St. Swithun's, and dedicated not only (like the old) to Saints Peter and Paul but also to Swithun, Bishop of Winchester in the years 852 to 862 and one of England's best-loved saints. He was a very English saint. That is to say he was loved and reverenced in his life for his sweetness of character and for his efficient and energetic conduct of business, and not because he was a mystic or a man who could work miracles. Indeed, there is record of only one miracle performed by Swithun in his lifetime. It is no very great miracle either. The Saint, we are told, moved by pity for an old dame who dropped her basket of eggs as she went to market, restored the eggs to her round and whole again. All the same, it is a very practical miracle; a very English miracle.

When Caxton printed his *Golden Legend* six hundred years after the Saint's death, he wrote of Swithun :

> " By his holy living he caused the people to live virtuously, and to pay truly their tithes to God and holy church. And if any church fell down or was in decay Saint Swithun would anon amend it at his own cost. Or if any church were not hallowed he would go thither on foot and hallow it. For he loved no pride nor to ride on gay horse, nor to be praised nor flattered of the people."

When Swithun came to die, adds Caxton, "he charged his men to bury him in the church-yard, for the people should not worship him after his death. For he loved no pomp by his life nor none would he have after his death." Of course the pomp and splendour he had refused in his lifetime claimed his bones in the end. A hundred years after his death, when the walls of the new Cathedral were rising on the foundations of the old, the earth over Swithun's bones was seen to heave and shake : a portent which was taken to mean that the Saint was pleading for reburial in the Cathedral. Perhaps the monks misinterpreted the signs. (More probably they were misled by their determination to install in their Cathedral a shrine which would attract a profitable press of pilgrims.) For when, on July 15, 971, Swithun's grave was opened, the heavens joined the remains of the Saint in a heavy, indeed a reckless, outburst of tears at this disregard of his last humble wishes. For forty days the rain poured down, and for forty days all that was mortal of the Saint lay under the sodden English summer sky awaiting translation.

Even those who know nothing else of Saint Swithun know of his continuing influence on the frequent miseries of the English summer. But the influence of the sweetness of his life is still fresh in Winchester. In a sense the whole Cathedral is his shrine. For nearly six hundred years countless Englishmen made their pilgrimage to pray before his relics for healing or for comfort of body and of mind. The shrine of the martyr-saint at Canterbury was not more reverenced in medieval times than that which housed Saint Swithun's bones.

These six hundred years of pilgrimage were also the years of Winchester's great days of glory as a capital city. Even when the less venerable city of London began to replace Winchester as the headquarters of the country's government, Winchester still held the affections of Englishmen as the cradle of their kings and the treasure-house of the legends of the heroic days of the birth of their nation. As late as 1485 a king who had won his crown on the field of battle saw to it that his heir was born in Winchester and christened in the Cathedral, so that the infant prince might inherit the traditions of the ancient city and its cathedral church.

It is these old and perhaps half-forgotten traditions which make Winchester Cathedral particularly precious among all the English cathedrals. No other has so rich a heritage from the distant past, and none so proud a story. In the shadow of its walls, or of the walls of the older buildings which preceded it, the destiny of the English-speaking races of the world was shaped. Here, more surely than from any other place in the world, is the place from which we come.

2 : *Norman Springtime*

WHEN the count of the English dead was made by the conquerors on the field of Hastings, there were found among the bodies those of a number of black-robed monks. Over their habits were suits of chain-mail. Their weapons lay by their sides, and their wounds were towards the invaders. When the news of the discovery was told to William, he said grimly : " The abbot is worth a barony, and each monk a manor."

The abbot and the monks who died at Hastings were of King Alfred's great religious foundation of New Minster at Winchester. They were not the last of Winchester's loyalist priests to fight for a losing cause ; but they were those who suffered most severely for their loyalties. Twenty thousand acres of the monastery lands were confiscated to fulfil William's promise made on the battlefield, and Alfred's great foundation at once ceased to be of any ecclesiastical importance.

The Old Minster, however, (the oldest of Winchester's several religious communities) absorbed the violent changes of the year of invasion without loss to its prestige or its wealth. Its monks remained neutral as William's army marched. William was crowned in the ancient Saxon cathedral two years after his coronation in London at a ceremony which the scribes declared was far more magnificent than the earlier one. It must have seemed to the monks of Old Minster that the whirlwind upon which the Normans were riding with the utmost confidence throughout Saxon England had passed them by. In fact the coronation of the Conqueror was the last of the great State ceremonies to take place in the ancient cathedral of the Saxon kings.

The Normans did not at once tear down the old building. But in 1079 they began the building of a new cathedral by its side. The man to whom we owe this, one of the largest medieval cathedrals in Europe, was Walkelin, Bishop of Winchester and kinsman of the King. The church that Walkelin built is substantially the Winchester Cathedral we know today. Substantially the same : the qualification is important. Inside and out great changes have been made to the Norman building. With the exception of some striking portions of the fabric, what we actually see at Winchester is not the work of Walkelin and his craftsmen. Yet the skeleton of this massive Cathedral is that which Walkelin planned and erected. Its severe, squat lines are Walkelin's. Its solid, earth-clinging hold on the floor of the Itchen valley is as striking a quality of its appearance today as it was to the traveller to Winchester nearly nine hundred years ago.

The scale of Walkelin's plans was majestic. Winchester was and remained, until the modern cathedral at Liverpool was begun, the longest cathedral in England. It is therefore astonishing that almost the entire building was said to have been erected within fourteen years. The achievement is, indeed, almost incredible if the imagination can re-create the conditions under which it was built : can see the workmen laboriously driving huge piles of timber into the marshes of the Itchen valley before ever a stone was laid ; can appreciate the appalling problems of building a huge crypt in the water-logged soil ; can visualize the crude tackle which hoisted tons of dressed stone (carried up the Itchen by boat from the Isle of Wight) to raise the walls ; and can hear for a moment the hum of the host of labourers and craftsmen who toiled to bring the work so swiftly to completion. Foresters, carters, masons, quarrymen, sailors, painters, stone-dressers, artificers of metal, labourers whose contribution was not skill but only the strength of their backs and arms—what force made them capable of so extraordinary an achievement ?

We know at least part of the answer. The human force was Walkelin's. The tribute to his drive and energy is retained in the old story of his collection of timbers for his cathedral. In his great need of wood, Walkelin approached the King who grudgingly (William was a fanatical hunter who hated to lose even a fraction of any of his grandiose coverts) allowed the Bishop as much wood as he could collect in four nights and days from Hempage Wood. It was sufficient a grant for Walkelin. He assembled every man he could find and marched his army to the wood. Within the allotted time the wood was as bare as if a swarm of locusts had settled in a field of young corn.

When William next rode out to his delectable wood, he swore profusely. One tree was left standing. It was a very aged oak under which Saint Augustine was once said to have preached the gospel.

Walkelin's Cathedral was then, as now, a cruciform building with a low and massive tower rising from the centre of the arms of the cross. But its exterior today is that of Norman times in spirit only. That is to say it is severe and harsh. It has something of the overmastering and self-keeping air of a fortress. It makes no concessions to those who think of cathedrals in terms of the soaring arch and spire ; those who expect cathedral walls to be an allegory in stone of Christianity's great aspirations ; or those who seek the satisfactions of the harmonious balances and tensions of mass and buttress, façade and pierced stone. The exterior is, in fact, a sad disappointment to anyone who goes to Winchester with pre-conceived ideas and ready-to-wear emotions.

Two points may therefore be made in explanation. Firstly, the new church was not built as the cathedral of a prince-bishop, nor to glorify God by its external beauty. It was built to serve as the priory church of a Benedictine foundation. Its plan was inspired first and last, by the rituals and ceremonies performed every arduous day of the lives of the monks who worshipped in it. All that was dramatic, or impressive, or that strengthened the effect of the monastic ritual was placed within the great and unadorned walls of the building.

Secondly, later bishops and master-builders considerably altered the Norman building —and not always for the better. If Walkelin's Cathedral had survived in its original form we should still have found it severe and forbidding. But we should certainly have conceded it an air of powerful majesty. Instead of the ineffective western entry we see today, Walkelin's building had a massive porch extending forty feet farther to the west. The great central entrance was flanked by two transepts topped by heavy square towers. Beyond the porch the walls of the long body of the church swept severely eastward to meet the arms of the transepts. The walls were strengthened by flat, utilitarian buttresses, and pierced by windows which, far from breaking the continuity of the stone, served rather (for they were compactly and frugally made) to emphasize the severity of the exterior.

At each corner of the transepts (where today are the lopped trunks of the towers on either side of the gables) were built heavy turrets. The shape and size of the central tower we do not know, for it collapsed a few years after it was completed. It was perhaps taller, and certainly even more severe, than the arcaded tower of the later Norman builders. Of the eastern part of the Norman cathedral nothing now remains. Later builders completely transformed it.

A splendid service to dedicate the Cathedral church of England's capital city was held on April 8, 1093. All the bishops and abbots of the country, the chronicle relates with pardonable exaggeration, were there to marvel at the vast building which gleamed, white and gold, on the green floor of the Itchen valley. By its side still stood the ancient and ramshackle Saxon cathedral—but not for much longer. A few weeks after the April ceremony of dedication, the bones of Saint Swithun were transferred to a shrine behind the high altar of the Norman church, and the Old Minster was demolished.

It is not difficult for the mind's eye to make this reconstruction of the Norman building. There is much to help the patient visitor if he will begin with the north transept whose grandeur has largely escaped the alterations of time. But it is *within* the north transept that the imagination is most free to grasp the nature of the Norman church and of the men who built it. Except for a few tombs, a few tablets on the walls, and the enclosure of one aisle to serve as a chapel, the north transept remains wholly the work of Walkelin's builders. Within it the structure of the entire Norman church is revealed, and we are at once brought, in an instant of astonishment, as near as we shall ever come to an understanding of the men who, for a brief moment of time, came down barbarians from the cold north, mastered the peoples and learned the ways of western Europe as far as the Mediterranean and beyond, and gave back to Europe an advance in culture and a rule of law that were all their own.

The impression is everywhere one of crushing power and strength. This architecture of squat piers relieved by the simplest of moulding, of rounded arches and of solid, round shaftings is without grace. It is masculine, vigorous, muscular and supremely confident. It is the style of a race of self-sufficient men in whose minds rose no shadow of a doubt about their destiny, and who were tormented by no questions of conduct, few scruples of conscience and no hesitations whatsoever. It is this quality of absolute conviction which separates us so profoundly from the Normans. We may envy it a little but we cannot share it. In the transepts of Winchester Cathedral we can even reject it as a quality too spare and too harsh to breed any of the humanities we hold desirable. It is grand, it is impressive, it is massive, it possesses tremendous authority and dignity. But it lacks entirely the supreme qualities that we have inherited from the civilization of Greece and through the mission of Jesus of Nazareth—the qualities of warmth and tenderness, of human delight and wonder at the preciousness of the individual man.

It is difficult (so powerful is the effect of William of Wykeham's vaulted nave) to imagine the entire Cathedral built in the style of the two transepts. But the body of the building was originally built to precisely the same plan. There were three storeys of almost equal but slightly diminishing height : above the pier arches were the double arches of the triforium gallery, and above these the windows of the clerestory. The roof was steep-pitched, and light came into the nave but thinly from the small windows in the aisles. The chief source of light was from the high windows in the clerestory some sixty feet from the floor of the nave.

Right across the church stood the screen or *pulpitum* which cut these monastic cathedrals into two compartments. Almost certainly the *pulpitum* was built one bay farther to the west than that spanned by the wooden choir screen today. On it hung the precious silver crucifix given to the Old Minster by Queen Emma, wife of the Saxon King Ethelred. The golden crown of Canute gleamed on the head of the crucified Son of God.

In this, the western half of the church, were held the public services and festivals of the Christian year. The eastern half (except for a pilgrim's way through the north transept to the shrine of Saint Swithun behind the high altar) was devoted to the rituals of the brothers of the Benedictine cloister. In the south transept (through which the monks passed to their daily services in the choir) were such church offices as the treasury.

Though the effect of the three tiers of arched storeys in which the Cathedral was built must have been heavy and forbidding, we must see the building as a stage on which were set forth, in ceremonies magnificently dressed, the great dramas of the Christian year. The galleries of the triforium, the passage which ran above the *pulpitum*, the aisles and the body of the nave were all the scenes of ritual processions in which coloured banners, gleaming relics and rich vestments glowed and flashed as they moved within the majestic setting which the Norman designers had provided for them. Moreover, in those days there existed no notion that stone should be left bare for the eye to appreciate its texture or the manner of its disposition in arch and pier. For hundreds of years a stone surface—whether that of a wall, a statue, or the ribs of a roof-vault—was considered a space suitable for decoration. So you may see in Winchester Cathedral, besides the several superb mural paintings that are among its glories, traces in the arches and vaults of the north transept of the colours and patterns which, from the Cathedral's earliest days, have enriched its walls.

When the Conqueror lay dying, his son hurried to Winchester to take possession of a treasure "hard to be numbered". It was a journey characteristic of the brief reign of William Rufus, whose record is one of ruthless self-interest and extortion of lands and revenues. Churchmen abominated him, and as it is largely on the judgments of monkish chroniclers that popular history has passed its verdict on Rufus, we can properly assume that he was hardly the supreme villain he was said to be. He was the type of money- and power-taking adventurer who rides the wave of a successful revolution. The wealth and power he demanded could be taken only from the Church ; it could certainly not come by extortion from his fellow-adventurers, the Norman barons. So bishoprics were left vacant and their revenues taken by the King. Church lands were made subject to feudal obligations. Grants of money were levied from monastic houses and wealthy prelates.

Even Walkelin's death was laid to the long account the Church was keeping of the Red King's villainies. In 1078, the story goes, Rufus sent Walkelin a demand for the then enormous sum of two hundred pounds. The Bishop " being unable to raise so large a sum without selling church valuables or robbing the poor, prayed that he might be delivered from the miseries of life." The Bishop's request was granted. He died full of years ten days later and was buried in the nave of his great Cathedral. To this same resting-place Rufus came within two years, riding meanly down to the Cathedral in a filthy two-wheeled forester's cart with Tyrell's arrow still in his heart.   "He was interred ", says the old account, " beneath the circuit of the tower with a concourse of many chiefs, but with the grief of few." He was the last King of England to be buried in Winchester Cathedral.

Where do the bones of Rufus now lie ? Are they among the bones in the mortuary chests one of which is inscribed (but in Latin) : " Here lie the bones of the Kings Canute and William Rufus " ? Or do they still rest under the simple, pointed roof of the Purbeck marble tomb which lies, without inscription, beneath the tower ? The answers to these questions are too involved for discussion here. It is most likely that the lovely stone in the choir does mark the burial place of the King. For, in 1868, the marble tomb was opened. In it was found the broken skeleton of a short and thickset man of middle years. With the bones were fragments of gold braid of Norman pattern, a small turquoise and the ivory head of a wand carved in the shape of a griffin. There were also found some pieces of wood and two small, angular pieces of iron. When fitted together they made an iron-tipped shaft nearly a yard long. Those who opened the tomb had, perhaps, reassembled the arrow which slew the Red King in the New Forest and which, according to an old record, was buried with the King still fast in his stiffened side.

Wherever the dust of Rufus now lies, he was certainly buried beneath the tower. For, seven years after his interment, a solemn sign was given to the faithful of displeasure that so profane a man should rest in so holy a place. With a portentous roar, the whole of Walkelin's tower collapsed upon the royal tomb. How complete was the tower's collapse can be judged from an inspection of the masonry of the reconstruction. If one stands facing west in the south transept, the shafts that frame the first compartment on the right of the triforium and clerestory are seen to be of very different workmanship. That nearer the tower is far smoother in finish : its texture is cleaner, the mortar between the stones is much narrower and more skilfully laid than that of the older pillar. The same neatness of construction may be observed in the fabric of the tower which was built with money left to the Cathedral by Walkelin, and was always known as "Walkelin's tower".

When they rebuilt it, the masons were taking no more chances. They enlarged the four already huge piers which supported it, and though they thus gave them an ungainly appearance as they are seen across the transepts, the builders preserved the grand view of the church from one end to the other by making the piers deeper from east to west than they are wide from north to south. Above the pillars, beyond the wooden vault which was added five hundred years later in the reign of Charles I, rose the magnificent lantern of the tower.

The tower of this Norman cathedral was not designed to raise a finger against the English sky, nor to house a peal of bells. Like the rest of the building, its duty was to enhance the richness and dignity of the worship of God within the walls. Through the lofty arched windows which pierce the four sides of what is now the bell-chamber, the light poured down to the floor of the choir far below. Many generations of monks lifted their eyes to this great lantern and saw the fickle English sunlight come and go among the distant mouldings, or marvelled at the shafts of golden light which reached down towards them as if they were the fingers of God himself. Many a devout brother caught in wonder at that high dance of light imprisoned within so lofty a space must have found the words to match his joy in the words of that serene and lovely psalm which reads : " Thy words are a lantern unto my feet ; and a light unto my path."

3 : *Early English*

"EVERY rich man built his castle," wrote a chronicler sourly of England's troubled years in the middle of the twelfth century, " and they filled the land full of castles ; and when the castles were finished they filled them with devils and evil men."

One of the most energetic of the castle-builders was Henry de Blois, Bishop of Winchester for forty-two violent and dismal years of English history. Had his years been passed in tranquil times, this ambitious man would certainly have been a great builder of churches and would have left his powerful mark on the fabric of Winchester Cathedral. As it was, he was principally a builder of castles. Only towards the end of his long life, all passion spent (and, it must be added, when he was quite out of favour with the new king Henry II), did he devote himself with humility to his see. Elsewhere he was responsible for some glorious churches. But to the structure of the Cathedral he added only the treasury in the south transept, beneath whose floor can be seen the pits which may once have held some of the Cathedral valuables. To de Blois the Cathedral also owes two of its most remarkable treasures : the black marble font which now stands in the nave, and the collection of the bones of Saxon kings and bishops which now rest in the mortuary chests on the screens of the choir near the high altar.

De Blois died in 1171. It is a date which can be said to mark a decisive step in the progress of the English story. Just as the death of de Blois was a reminder that the days of lawless individualism were over, so the reign of Henry II was proof that the rule of anarchy was yielding to the rule of law.

" Before this sovereign," says H. A. L. Fisher, " whose brilliant power of thought and action amounted to genius, had finished his work, royal judges were going on assize as they have ever since continued to do, representing the authority of the king and the majesty of the law, the jury was fast superseding archaic methods of proof, such as the ordeal and the duel, and the king had established his position as fountain of justice and guardian of the public peace. Racialism was dead."[1]

Racialism was dead. Somewhere towards the turn of the twelfth century the miracle was achieved. This island ceased to be a country plagued by a division between Norman conquerors and Saxon conquered. Imperceptibly the invaders had been absorbed by the character of the English countryside and of its easy-going but tenacious folk. Gradually the Saxon tongue was mingling with the Norman. The country became a unity. It became *England*.

The proof of this transformation is dramatically made within the walls of Winchester Cathedral. It lies around the visitor when he passes out of the Norman transepts into the east end of the church and stands in the retrochoir. The change is astonishing. We are in entirely another world of thought and feeling. At no point whatsoever are the architects, between whom lies only a century of time, on common ground. The rounded arch has given way to a pointed arch of exquisite simplicity. Graceful arcaded panels decorate walls that earlier were bare of embellishment. Slender shafts, widely spaced, have replaced the squat and close-set piers. The rough barrel vault and rudimentary roofing ribs have gone. In their place are vaults as taut as the arch of a stretched bow. Massiveness has vanished and modesty of scale has taken its place. Where one style is oppressive and somehow menacing, this is as fresh and gay and clear-cut as a morning in springtime. The light is welcome here. It is to be enjoyed. One feels, within the spaces enclosed by these slender shafts of stone, the same sense of freedom as lifts the heart in a plantation of straight young trees which in time enough will grow old and dignified but which now let in the breezes and the sunlight.

Everywhere in England at this time the builders were thus undoing or adding to the work of the Norman craftsmen. Nowhere else in Europe was there a similar expression in stone of this consciousness of youth, of springtime, and of a new spirit of nationhood. This style, this very sweet and very gracious way with stone, was peculiar to England—a wonderful memorial to the moment in our history which marked the birth of our nation.

The reconstruction of the retrochoir was the work of de Lucy, Bishop of Winchester from 1188 to 1204. The manner of the work of reconstruction was simple. Around the east end of the Norman structure (which ended in a small, rounded chapel built on the foundation of the crypt) de Lucy built the outer walls of his extension and carried them straight out from the lines of the walls of the Norman choir. The east end was built straight from north to south and formed the rear wall of three chapels of equal size. (The extent of the later addition to the central chapel of the three, the Lady Chapel, is clearly marked by the abrupt ending, halfway down its length, of de Lucy's lovely arcading.) When the outer walls were finished the columns in the centre of the retrochoir which support the vaulted roof were erected on the foundation of the Norman crypt.

The work was completed by the laying of a floor of encaustic tiles, many of which— of delicate design—still remain in a floor which, in six centuries, has so sunk and settled that it has the texture and unexpected contours of an old carpet that has been blown about by a sudden draught. In the south-west corner of the Cathedral, indeed, the floor slips surprisingly away from its proper level. So do the walls, which lean at most unorthodox angles. At this place the old timber piles of the foundations rotted away and great gaps were torn in recent times in de Lucy's roofs. It is a vivid reminder of the difficulties the Norman builders encountered when they decided to build on a marsh.

We do not know, for all the monastic records have been destroyed, who first undertook the task of rebuilding the old Norman choir and of joining it to the retrochoir. The work

[1] *A History of Europe.* H. A. L. Fisher. Edward Arnold, 1936.

was probably begun in the time of Bishop Woodlock, a hundred years after de Lucy's death, for there is evidence that the carving of the glorious choir stalls was begun in 1308 and their installation was probably part of a larger plan of reconstruction in this part of the church.   As de Lucy had done in the retrochoir, the builder of the bold arches of the presbytery erected them upon the foundations of the Norman crypt.   To effect a reasonable junction between retrochoir and presbytery, he drew the two easternmost pillars closer together than were their fellows.   This explains the polygonal shape of the feretory behind the high altar.   Within the feretory can be seen the solutions that a succession of builders sought to make of the problems left to them by de Lucy.   The arches spring from various levels.   They interpenetrate in a highly unorthodox fashion.   The shafts that support them and the abacuses on which they rest are of different heights.   There is even the stump of one of the old Norman choir pillars left jutting from the floor of Gardiner's chantry as though the builders had finally abandoned the reconstruction in despair.   In short, there exists in this part of the Cathedral a fine architectural confusion.

The purpose of de Lucy's reconstruction of the east end of the Cathedral was not, as some writers have said, to make a greater space for the pilgrims who were at this time crowding to the shrine of Saint Swithun.   It was to provide more worthily for the worship of Our Lady whose importance in the devotions of the cloister was now increasing.   Nevertheless, the effect of the reconstruction was to open up a clear passage for the pilgrims and to make the shrine of the Saint far more accessible than it had been hitherto.

We cannot now say beyond a doubt what was the position of this famous shrine.   We know for certain that it was placed behind the high altar.   Some historians have placed it in the feretory where, in 1922, there were found fragments of Purbeck marble which may have formed the base of the shrine.   The most probable site is that which is marked by a border of Hopton Wood stone in the centre of the retrochoir.   In one of the roof bosses above the site is a hole which may once have held a pulley to raise the lid of the shrine ; and until recently a shallow trough was to be seen worn in the tiled floor west of the Wayneflete and Beaufort chantries as if the feet and knees of countless people had fretted away the brick as they made their devotions.   Around the site of the shrine runs a Latin inscription whose translation is :

> " All of St. Swithun that could die lay here enshrined.   Hither came the faithful, not of one age or clime, to honour him with prayers and gifts.   A later age laid rude hands upon his relics but could not touch his fame.   All that is of God is safe in God."[1]

We can make a reasonable guess at the route the faithful took to honour the Saint. Their entry was certainly on the north side of the Cathedral, for the south transept and the choir were places trodden only by the brethren of the Priory.   We know that the north transept was occupied by booths for the sale of candles and relics, and we can see today in the west face of the north transept a blocked-up doorway which would have been the most suitable point of entry for pilgrims in the Cathedral.   The traveller entering by this door came into a transept whose walls blazed with colour.   On the opposite wall, where there is still a dark angular shadow above the tablet to the memory of S. S. Wesley, he may have seen an image of Saint Christopher, patron saint of travellers, and beneath it a box for the gift of alms.   Buying a candle on his way, the traveller probably lit it from a taper burning behind the quatrefoil embrasure in the wall of the Chapel of the Holy Sepulchre.   He passed up the steps into the presbytery aisle and made his slow progress with the crowd into the retrochoir where stood the object of his search and the end of his long and often painful journey.

It was an astonishing and impressive sight.   The shrine was raised high above the ground upon a grey marble base.   Above it hung a lifted canopy, brilliantly coloured. On the richly carved casket of silver and gold which contained the Saint's bones there

[1] Translation by Canon A. W. Goodman in *Winchester Cathedral Record* No. 6.   1937.

gleamed and danced the starry fires of jewels and of the reflections of the scores of candles carried by the pilgrims.   Crutches and sticks discarded by those to whom the marvel of a cure had been granted hung from the sides of the shrine.   Around it clustered the pitiful wrecks of men and women and children thrusting their diseased limbs or their tormented bodies against the surface of the shrine in the hope that this touch would make them whole. Among them knelt the perhaps more fortunate whose sickness was of the heart or mind, and those who were troubled by nothing, but whose hearts were light in the fulfilment of a pious oath and of a journey.

The monks quite properly separated themselves from the pilgrims.   Across the east entry to the south transept stood the superb iron gates that still stand there today.   A screen was erected behind the high altar not only so that its west face should glorify the splendour of the new presbytery but also to shut off the noise and view of the crowds from the brethren at their devotions.   In an age without benefit of the science of medicine, the sight of the sick was, of course, distracting to a sensitive mind.

4 : *Gothic Glory*

IF the pilgrim to Winchester Cathedral is disappointed by its external appearance or by the modesty of its setting within the buildings of the town, he will be the more moved by the grandeur that is revealed to him when he enters the west door and stands within the nave.

For, surprisingly, the nave contradicts and obliterates from the mind the sense of a building squat and heavy in appearance.   The impression is overwhelmingly one of height, and of great space which spreads out far to the window above the high altar and is, it seems, barely confined by the stone vault which hangs high overhead.   Light fills this great vault.   It pours in from the clerestory windows which are completely hidden by the massive pillars—so massive that from the west end of the nave no source of light is seen save from the window immediately to the right and from the graceful window which crowns the reredos high in the east wall.

It is this sense of light omnipresent but of invisible entry which is the supreme quality of this wonderful nave.   The walls which from outside looked so unpromising have within become as screens through which pours a radiance giving to the old stone a veil of colour of the palest lilac.   From whatever point the nave is seen there is the same dramatic invitation to the light of day.   Looking down the nave from the top of the reredos, the west window appears to fill the entire wall, to empty it of weight, and to make of it no more a barrier to the sky than are the branches of a tree under the summer sun.   Or, standing beneath this window, one may marvel at the high-hung east window the curves of whose arches hold so subtle a balance between the tense angles of the vault and the leisurely Norman curves of the tower arches.   Light is flung down in the distance into a well of space behind the reredos, creating a sense as of a reaching out into the infinite and yet—by a master stroke of design—drawing the eye to a point of rest upon the reredos which stands out, detached from its background, to close the east wall of the Cathedral's heart—the high altar.

Architecturally, the Cathedral nave is one of the most glorious examples of Gothic building in England.   In it are combined with dramatic intensity the two outstanding, and apparently contradictory, qualities of Gothic architecture : its tension and its serenity.

The ribs of the vault of Winchester's nave spring from their supporting piers with the urgency of an arrow driven from a bow.   The line of their flight on either side is swift and vigorous. They are not concerned to conceal the strain of the great weight of the stone canopy they uphold : rather, they emphasize it and, doing so, turn the play of mere mechanical forces into a drama of the struggle of great stresses to burst free from the counterthrusts which hold them in check. This vault is as if alive. Through its ribs and tracery there flows a vital sap. It is as restless, yet it is as serenely majestic, as is the head of a great tree. It explains why Gothic architecture conveys to many the exhilaration and grandeur of an army swiftly on the march bearing its banners and a glitter of uplifted spears.

Yet the lasting impression that the nave conveys is one not of movement but of tranquillity. It is possible to analyse the reasons why this should be so : how, for instance, the enormous piers which take the weight of the vault drain its tensions away into the floor beneath ; and how the perspective of the nave appears to recede remotely into and beyond the light of the east window. When all the reasons have been stated, however, and the sum is struck, we are left to marvel at a magic which is beyond computation. The nave is, indeed, as serene and seemingly as inevitable as a work of nature.

So impressive is the nave that it is hardly credible that it was once built in the forbidding style of the transepts. It is still more difficult to believe that the very stones of the massive piers—many of them still visible—are those that Walkelin's craftsmen carried to the site from anchorages on the Itchen. Yet it is true, and it is an added marvel, that the nave was not the work of an architect free to build as he desired, but a reconstruction, pier by pier and bay by bay, of the existing Norman fabric.

The bishops who directed and financed the transformation of the nave were William of Edington and William of Wykeham. Of the two, Wykeham was the greater man and by far the nobler builder. But it was Edington who began the work, and it was Edington who chose Wykeham as a young man to be his secretary and who was the architect of Wykeham's splendid career.

It is well to remember these facts, for the truth is that Edington was himself a dull and uninspired builder whose legacies to the structure of the Cathedral are not among its glories.

Like many of the great medieval prelates, Edington was trained as a civil servant whose salary as Lord Treasurer of England was provided by rapid preferment in the hierarchy of the Church. This method of rewarding civil servants may seem odd to us ; but it was inevitable in days when kings had no organized system of taxes with which to finance their administration, and when practically all educated men were monks or in the service of the Church. Where else could the king turn for skilled administrators but to the Church ? Or how else reward his outstanding laymen than by appointing them to wealthy benefices ? Wykeham, for instance, was forty before he was ordained priest, and even before his ordination (he served the King as Surveyor of the Royal Castles and Keeper of the Privy Seal) had drawn the revenues of many rich appointments in the Church.

Edington began his task of reconstruction by destroying Walkelin's great Norman porch and using many of its stones to pave the Winchester streets. The west front he built in its place is a poor compensation for what was lost. Except that, from within, the west window wonderfully fulfils its purpose of flooding the nave with light, and that from without it provides the student with an admirably severe example of the Early Perpendicular style, there is little to be said in favour of Winchester's west front. It looks what, in fact, it is: a huge façade which is propped (like a piece of theatre scenery on a back-stage wall) against the body of the nave.

Edington's reconstruction in the nave was hardly more inspired than was his west front. Fortunately he built little more than two windows in the north aisle and one in the south, and the striking difference between the quality of the work of Edington and Wykeham can best be seen on the exterior wall of the north aisle at its west end.   The two westernmost windows are sadly placed within the frame of buttresses.   They are too large and too deep for their setting.   The moulding is heavy and over-powerful.   The effect they produce is one of gloom, not of an invitation to the light.   The window next to them, however, (which is the work of Wykeham's architects) makes use of similar elements of design but so refines and readjusts them to their surroundings that the effect is one of simple grace and dignity.

When Wykeham began to reconstruct the nave towards the end of his long and splendid life of service to the Church and to the State his architects worked strictly within the frame of the design of the Norman builders.   They began by tearing out the arcading of the triforium and the lower arches which supported it.   They lifted the pointed arches high towards the heads of the piers and surmounted them with a line of delicately moulded balconies.   The tiny Romanesque windows of the clerestory were enlarged and the old stone below them faced with moulded panels.   The sturdy piers were refined by cutting into their square or rounded corners the exquisite moulding we see today, whose duty is to conceal the gross mass of stone of which they are composed, and to draw the eye upward to the superb vault of the roof.

It is of interest that when the work began on the columns of the south side of the nave, they were taken down stone by stone and re-cut before they were re-placed.   Eight columns were so treated, for these eight westernmost columns show the thick and clumsy Norman mortaring.   The method was slow and probably dangerous.   It was not used on the other columns which were re-faced with new stone.   Only the cores of these columns are of Norman workmanship.

The crown of Wykeham's work was the replacement of the steep-pitched timber roof of the old church by the great stone vault we have already described.   It is, as are all these Gothic canopies of stone, a marvel of engineering.   Its tremendous weight is supported by the short ribs (or *liernes*) which knit the main arch-ribs together and which, in turn, transfer the weight to the shafts beneath.   The Winchester architects did not make use of the exterior flying buttresses with which most other Gothic builders strengthened their audacious buildings and wonderfully enhanced their beauty.   They constructed instead small flying buttresses above the vaults of the aisles and so transferred some of the weight of the aisle vault to the Cathedral's outer walls.   It was not a sound procedure. In later centuries the strains told and the south wall began to show signs of giving way. At last, in 1912, five centuries after the vault was built, true flying buttresses were constructed to support the south wall.   They are competently made.   They undoubtedly perform the task for which they were designed.   Alas, the secret of which the Gothic builders were masters and which turned even the details of their structures into imperishable works of art, remained unrevealed to the builders of the twentieth century.

Edington and Wykeham both chose to lie when they were dead in the nave they left to us as their memorial.   To Wykeham (who like so many poor men's sons who have made great names for themselves by their own wit and energy, burned to provide for other boys without means the education he had missed himself) we also owe the foundations of Winchester College and New College at Oxford.   But it was the Cathedral he glorified that was his earliest and his last love.

When he was a child, he used to lean against one of the pillars on the south side of the nave and there watch the splendid rituals and ceremonies of the Christian year.   When he was old it was to the foot of this same pillar that he desired to be carried at his death.

Just such a boy as the young Wykeham—a boy receiving in Winchester the benefit of the bishop's passion that " the strength of the Christian religion grow hotter and all knowledge and virtue be increased in strength "—leaned nearly two hundred years later against a pillar two bays above that occupied by Wykeham's chantry. As boys will, he took a nail from his pocket and wrote upon the stone :

Jhon Hassall
Childe of Win
chester colledg
1588

If the spirit of Wykeham was witness, it would have pardoned this venial act of vandalism. Indeed it would, for very many reasons, have been moved to that joy whose laughter is so very near to tears.

5 : *The House Completed*

WYKEHAM'S work on the nave was begun in 1394. From that time until the splendid age of cathedral building was brought to an abrupt end by Henry VIII's dissolution of the monastic system, reconstruction of Winchester Cathedral was almost continuous. Many of the Cathedral's most exquisite architectural treasures were added to it during the fifteenth century, and these stones suggest an ordered peace in which the arts were free to flourish and men enjoyed a breathing space of liberty and prosperity.

In fact, the century was politically far from peaceful. Most of its years were consumed by the miseries of civil wars. Powerful feudal lords set themselves above the law by equipping themselves with private armies, and kings sat uneasily on their thrones. Winchester, however, was curiously fortunate in the longevity of its bishops. While England had nine kings, Winchester was ruled by only three bishops. Wykeham held the see for thirty-eight years, Beaufort for forty-three and Wayneflete for nearly forty more. Thus, though all three were Lords Chancellor of the kingdom and Beaufort especially was little seen in his diocese, the Cathedral developed under an administration which suffered few interruptions.

Beaufort's beginnings were vastly different from those of the poor yeoman's son Wykeham ; he was the illegitimate son of John of Gaunt and Katherine Swynford, and therefore of royal blood. He was made Bishop of Winchester at the age of twenty-eight and was shortly afterwards rewarded for political services to the Pope by the award of the Cardinal's hat. His career was that of a prince, a statesman, a soldier, and a nobleman of vast wealth, who was deeply involved in the squalid political manœuvres of his times.

During Beaufort's tenure of the see, Wykeham's nave vault was probably completed. It is certain, in any event, that much of the building was done in his time, for among the vault bosses and corbels in the nave are Beaufort's arms (England quartering France) and the white hart chained which was the device of Richard II, Beaufort's cousin. It is also likely that work on the nave as a whole was not brought to an end until well into the rule of Beaufort's successor, William of Wayneflete, whose device of a lily (his arms are to this day those of Eton and of Magdalen College) is also to be seen in the nave.

Wayneflete was, like Wykeham, the son of poor parents, and a great educator. He was headmaster of Winchester College and afterwards first Provost of Henry VI's new foundation of Eton College. When Beaufort died Wayneflete became Bishop of Winchester and Henry's Lord Chancellor. He just outlived the last act of the Wars of the Roses, dying a year after Henry VII's victory at Bosworth Field in 1487.

It was due to Henry Tudor's sense of his insecurity as a usurper of the throne that the Cathedral owes the next significant addition to its fabric. By every possible means Henry was determined to create an impression of legitimacy for the royal line of which he was the founder. When the time of the birth of his heir approached, Queen Elizabeth was therefore sent to Winchester so that her child could be declared a true inheritor of all the ancient royal traditions of the city. The boy-child was born in St. Swithun's Priory in 1491. Henry exerted himself to improve the occasion. Many great noblemen and state officials were summoned to the gorgeously decorated church. There was much singing of Te Deums and ringing of bells. Bonfires were lit about the town and two pipes of wine (" that every Man myght drynke ynow ") were broached in the churchyard. When the little prince was dipped into the black marble font of Bishop de Blois, the name spoken over his damp head was that of King Arthur, whose glorious company (so every citizen of Winchester believed) had once made the city its headquarters. Henceforward, there was to be no doubt that the young prince was legitimately heir to all that was best and most romantic in the English story.

Arthur did not, however, live beyond his sixteenth year. But the addition made to the Lady Chapel at its east end remains as a memorial of the ceremony of his christening. Elizabeth of York made a gift of money to Prior Hunton as a thank-offering for the birth of her child. The extension of the Cathedral made possible by the gift, makes Winchester the longest pre-Reformation cathedral in the world. Its internal length is just over 526 feet.

The addition built by Hunton's architects makes no attempt to copy the simple and lovely arcading of de Lucy. The extension was put up, indeed, as if the builders had no notion that pedants might one day criticize so surprising a mixture of styles. They simply added their elaborate walls to the old fabric, and (if they worried about it at all) left the verdict to time. Few people are likely to quarrel with the result. Each half of the chapel is lovely ; each retains its identity and the stamp of the craftsmen who made it without loss to the harmony of the whole. The simplicity of one and the rich elaboration of the other, have come happily together as all things that are lovely must in the passage of time.

When Richard Fox was translated from the see of Exeter to that of Winchester in 1500 a partnership began between the Bishop and Silkstede, Prior of St. Swithun's, which lasted nearly twenty-five years and which created some of the Cathedral's loveliest treasures. None of the work these men undertook is of massive scale. But all of it is rich and delicate, as if touched by the glowing light of the Indian summer of the Old Faith, so soon to end in the storms of the spoliation of the monasteries and the victory of the reformers. And, as if instinct warned the Bishop and his Prior that time was precious, the construction they put in hand was precisely that which made the great Cathedral a unity : which, busying itself with the presbytery and choir, joined new nave to older retrochoir, and left the transepts to speak for the men who were the Cathedral's founders. Under their direction in this quarter of a century the presbytery was enclosed, the clerestory of the choir constructed and its magnificent flying buttresses hung above the east walls ; the wooden vault was built above the choir, the reredos completed, and the east window above it built and filled with glowing stained glass.

The effect of Fox's east window on the appearance of the nave has already been discussed. Like all of his work, it is one of those architectural details whose value to the fabric of the whole is even greater than its own merits ; greater, perhaps, than the builders themselves knew. Those who climb on to the leaded roof of the retrochoir can see what are probably portrait heads of Fox and his friend and master, Henry VII. The label of the east window springs from two corbels of a king and a bishop. From this vantage point, too, Fox's perfect flying buttresses (erected to support the presbytery walls) can best be seen. The moulding of the stone is, though much worn by time, of great beauty. It includes the device of the pelican in her piety which Fox displayed on his arms. This pious bird (which is represented in legend as tearing her breast with her beak so that her young might feed on her blood, and which, therefore, became a medieval symbol of the Passion) is carved into all of Fox's work. There is a vividly realistic version, for instance, in the Bishop's coat of arms which hangs among the unique series of wooden bosses of the presbytery vault.

This vault is a structure of astonishing virtuosity, and was built of wood because the presbytery walls would not have supported the weight of a stone roof. The carpenters hung this great canopy between the walls entirely without the use of nails. As anyone can see who walks above it, its timbers are held together by wooden pegs—and by superb and devoted craftsmanship. The resemblance of the structure to the true stone vault was completed by hanging a series of sham wooden bosses at the junctions of the ribs. They serve a decorative purpose only, whereas, of course, the bosses of Gothic stone vaults are the decorated faces of the roof's essential keystones. The bosses above the presbytery may offend the purist, but will offend few others. They form a unique collection of boldly constructed heraldic devices, half of which (at the west end) are of kings and princes, bishops and noble families, and half, above the high altar, of the heraldry of the Passion. The latter is the most comprehensive of its kind in England. It is executed with the same naive realism as are the Passion emblems which are still to be seen on the roadside Calvaries of Southern Europe. The strict formalism of the heraldic expert has been imposed upon this naivety, with results that are, in places, startling. Among the several brightly coloured shields are those showing a sword in the act of taking off Malchus's ear, a head of a Jew spitting, the cup of vinegar, the heads of Pilate and his wife, a pair of dice, a Veronica, and the many instruments of the Crucifixion. The collection is the most curious and most striking memorial of the last days of the Age of Faith that any English cathedral possesses.

There are several impressive bosses in the west half of the vault. Among them are badges of the Saxon kings, arms of the see of Winchester, of Richard Fox and of Henry Tudor. Like the Passion emblems, some of them ingeniously tell a story. One device, for instance, displays the hawthorn bush (its blossoms and the texture of its bark are of vivid realism) from which Henry Tudor picked the abandoned crown of England on Bosworth Field. On either side of the bush, which is surmounted by the crown, the initials H. R. (Henricus Rex) are cunningly contrived from the Welsh dragon and pieces of horse furniture.

The stone screens with which Fox enclosed the presbytery must have been built towards the end of his life. Not only are they of the same delicate workmanship as his marvellous chantry, but they also bear a label with the initials H.B., which were those of Prior Henry Brook who succeeded Silkstede in 1524. The screens hang beneath the lovely Early English arches of the presbytery aisles. Arches and screens share the same restraint, the same fragility of line, the same dignity. With the reredos, they form an enclosure for the space before the high altar whose beauty is nowhere surpassed in any of the medieval cathedrals.

When the screens were finished, Fox placed above the Italianate frieze which surmounts them the six chests he had had made by his Italian workmen to receive the bones of the Saxon kings and bishops that were collected by de Blois. Like the bosses on the vault above them, they are vivid memorials to the lively imagination and the devoted energy of a bishop to whom the Cathedral owes much.

There is one more curious legacy of this time. In the gable of the north transept is a large rose-window of unusual design. The three double bars of stone which lie across the diameter of the circle look like a geometrical exercise worked out in masonry. But the mystery is that this window can neither be seen from within nor gives any light whatsoever to the transept. Behind it is nothing but a mass of roof timbers.

For what reason was this surprising window built ? The only reasonable explanation seems to be that Fox or his architects felt that the exterior of the Cathedral needed enlivening, and that it would please the citizens to have, as it were, an eye looking into the Cathedral as they went about their business in Winchester's streets.

6 : *Glory Departed*

WHATEVER balance is struck between the social gains and losses caused to the country by the Reformation, it is beyond argument that the loss to our heritage of the work of the medieval architects and craftsmen is absolute. The record is one of robbery and destruction under the law which, carried a stage farther in the Civil War a hundred years later, lost us an artistic treasure too rich to be calculated.

Winchester, the wealthiest see in England, could not expect to avoid expropriations. It had always been much coveted by kings hard-pressed for money and by ambitious churchmen. It was therefore natural that when Richard Fox died in 1528 Wolsey should add its great revenues to his already enormous income. The most insatiable pluralist in the history of the Church, Wolsey did not once trouble to visit Winchester during his brief bishopric. He was even installed by proxy. His interest in his diocese was purely financial. He spent its revenues, and the money he obtained from breaking up some of its monasteries, on the colleges he was building as a sign of his magnificence.

The dissolution of the smaller monasteries began in 1535. The greater religious houses—among them the Priory of St. Swithun's and its cathedral church—were dissolved by Act of Parliament in 1539. A year before, however, Thomas Cromwell's Commissioners had already visited Winchester to despoil it of its realizable treasure under cover of the hypocritical excuse that the relics and shrines were " the abomination of idolatry". A remarkable report of this visitation exists under the signatures of the Commissioners Pollard, Wriothesly and Williams, which reads :

"Pleaseth your lordship to be advertized, that this Saturday in the morning, about three of the clock, we made an end of the shrine [1] here in Winchester. There was in it no piece of gold, nor one ring, or true stone, but all great counterfeits. Nevertheless we think the silver alone thereof will amount near to two thousand marks. We have also received into our possession the cross of emeralds, the cross called Jerusalem, another cross of gold, two chalices of gold, with some silver plate, parcel of the portion of the vestry ; but the old prior made the plate of the house so thin, that we can diminish none of it and leave the prior anything furnished.

"We found the prior and all the convent very conformable ; having assistants with us . . . . . who, with one voice most heartily gave laud and praise to God and to the King's majesty, thinking verily that they do all as much rejoice of his majesty's godly and most Christian purpose herein as can be devised.

"We have also this morning, going to our beds-ward, viewed the altar, which we purpose to bring with us. It will be worth taking down, and nothing thereof seen ; but such a piece of work it is, that we think we shall not rid it, doing our best, before Monday night or Tuesday morning, which done, we intend both at Hide and St. Mary's, to sweep away all the rotten bones that be called relics ; which we may not omit, lest it be thought we came more for the treasure than for avoiding of the abomination of idolatry. Other things, as far as we can learn, there be none for us in those places . . . . ." [2]

A more cynical document or one which more clearly reveals some of the motives behind Cromwell's spoliation of the Church it is impossible to imagine. Everything of value that could be moved by the wretched Commissioners was carried away, and, that the gullible

---

[1] That is, the shrine of St. Swithun.
[2] Extracts from a version quoted in *Historic Winchester*, A. R. Bramston and A. C. Leroy ; Longmans, Green & Co. 1882.

should be provided with reason for the thefts, priceless images were destroyed, shrines smashed, and the relics of the saints scattered.

We do not know the full sum of the Cathedral's losses. In addition to those treasures described in the Commissioners' letter, there were also taken the golden crown which Canute had hung, in an act of humility, above the crucifix of the high altar ; the magnificent silver and gilt crucifix with its attendant figures of the Virgin and Saint John which was the gift, in the eleventh century, of Bishop Stigand ; images decorated in jewels and precious stones which stood on the reredos and in the chantries of the builder-bishops ; and many tapestries which hung on the walls. Even the brasses and inscriptions on several tombstones were cut away. Perhaps the best indication of the thoroughness of the work of destruction is the fact that when the Cathedral was handed back in 1541, not to a prior of St. Swithun's, but to the newly-styled Dean and his Chapter, not a single wall monument remained in the Cathedral. The splendour that had taken nearly five centuries in the making was extinguished. The glory had departed.

The Prior who was described in the Commissioners' report as " very conformable " was William Kingsmill, last Prior of St. Swithun's and first Dean of the Chapter of Winchester Cathedral. His conformity to the outrageous destruction of the treasures in his care is understandable. Gardiner, who was appointed Bishop of Winchester after Wolsey's death, was whole-heartedly the King's man : that is to say, he was as strong for the rejection of the supremacy of the Pope as he was urgent in the persecution of those who held dissenting opinions on the doctrines of the Catholic Faith. He was, as were many of the old bishops, no great lover of monks, and was anxious that, through the dissolution of the monasteries, there should be a great increase throughout the country of secular education.

In Henry VIII's Statutes for Winchester Cathedral inaugurating the new order (which Gardiner must have helped to frame), it is stated that St. Swithun's Monastery is dissolved in order that " where ignorance and superstition used to reign the sincere worship of God may flourish, and the Gospel be diligently preached in its purity ; and also that, to the advancement of the Christian Faith and of piety, the youth of the realm may be educated in good letters ". The motives were not, of course, so lofty as they appeared in the Statutes. The transaction was a profitable one for the King to whose appropriately named Court of Augmentations the revenues of the see of Winchester were handed over. Kingsmill the Dean eventually disposed of considerably smaller revenues than those that were available to his predecessor, Kingsmill the Prior.

About no other English bishop has more violent or more partisan literature been written than about Stephen Gardiner. To Protestants he was the devil himself, for he was the author of the punitive Six Articles of Henry VIII and the ruthless hunter of the martyrs who went to the stake during the Marian persecutions. Gardiner possessed at least the merit of consistency in his refusal to compromise with the doctrines of reform. In the reign of Edward VI he was imprisoned for five years in the Tower of London and deprived of his see, because he would not reject the doctrines of the Old Faith. Released almost as soon as Mary came to the throne, he was re-installed as Bishop of Winchester and appointed Lord Chancellor of England. For the next five unhappy years the country was under the rule of two bitter, angry people whose persecution of the " heretics " did as much as anything to establish the Protestant faith in English hearts and emotions. Winchester was spared most of the horrors of the religious persecution. The city was as loyalist in feeling as ever. Only one burning was witnessed in its streets in those days. It was, moreover, the scene of Mary's tragi-comical marriage to Philip of Spain in 1554.

The unhappy Spaniards, pallid from their sea-journey, were drenched by a great storm of rain on their journey from Southampton, but they were said to have been impressed by the Cathedral and surprised that barbarians who were brutish enough to survive the rigours of so evil a climate could sing a Mass as handsomely as did the choirs of Toledo.

The marriage ceremony was a magnificent one. The Queen so blazed with jewels (which included the famous pearl *La Pelegrina*) that " the eye was blinded as it looked upon her ". The Prince was arrayed in cloth of gold. The splendid robes of six bishops glittered in the light of the candles. Trumpets were sounded as the royal pair advanced to the high altar to celebrate Mass after they had made their marriage vows. The ceremony lasted from eleven o'clock in the morning to three o'clock in the afternoon, and was promptly followed by a dinner at which scholars of Winchester College recited interminable eulogies in Latin. The indefatigable company (Philip alone was said to have brought four thousand followers with him) then danced far into the evening. Two memorials of this ceremony survive in Winchester Cathedral. The iron brackets on the pillars of the nave are said to have been put there to hold the tapestries and embroidered cloths used to decorate the nave at the wedding. The Cathedral also possesses the chair on which Mary sat during the long ceremonies of a marriage which brought her no political advantages and great personal unhappiness.

Gardiner died in London in 1555, shortly after the death of the Queen he had striven to serve after his fashion. Three months later he set out on his last princely journey to his Cathedral church, lying on a chariot drawn by four sable-draped horses. A waxen figure of the Bishop lay on the coffin, dressed in the dead man's most splendid priestly robes. Behind the chariot walked a company of four hundred priests and servants bearing torches or smoking censers. At every village the procession halted and Masses and dirges were sung until, at last, the procession reached Winchester where the coffin was carried to the chantry that awaited it. Such was the manner of the burial of the last of Winchester's medieval statesmen-bishops. The *post mortem* rites later accorded to the Bishop by the people were, however, less splendid. The stone cadaver of Stephen Gardiner which lay in a niche in the face of his chantry was attacked with axes and hammers. So violent was popular feeling that the stone head was torn away from the body.

During the next half century the Cathedral was in decay. More of its images were stripped by reforming bishops. Until recent research proved the accusation false,[1] it was always assumed that Robert Horne, Bishop of Winchester from 1560-80, was responsible for stripping the Cathedral roofs of lead for his own profit, and for the destruction of the cloisters and the chapter house. In fact, the chapter house was pulled down in 1637 on the eve of the Civil War which was once more to enlarge the grievous sum of the Cathedral's losses. Before the war broke out, however, one notable addition was made to the Cathedral. Inigo Jones was given the task of designing a vault at the base of the tower, above the choir. His model was the roof of Winchester College chapel, and, like that of Fox's presbytery, it was carried out in wood. The wood masquerades as stone, but it is none the less a delicately lovely work. It bears among its bosses the arms and devices of Charles I and his wife and their medallion portraits, the arms of Scotland and Ireland, and the devices of ecclesiastics of the day. In the centre is an emblem of the Trinity girdled by an ingenious inscription which reads :

> SInt DoMUs hUIUs pII reges nUtrItII
> regInae nUtrICes pIae
> (May pious kings and queens nourish this church.)

The larger letters are painted in red. When they are rearranged they make an equivalent of the date in Latin numerals of the year, 1635, of the roof's erection.

True to its loyalist traditions, Winchester was for the King when the Civil War broke out. The city changed hands more than once during the fighting and was besieged in 1645 by Cromwell himself who shortly took it and blew up the castle.

[1] See *Cathedral Record* No. 10, 1941; Canon A. W. Goodman.

The Cathedral had by this time suffered from the zeal of the parliamentarians—notably on a December morning in 1642 when

> " the soldiers of the Parliament entered the Cathedral with colours flying, their drums beating, and their matches fired. Some of their Troops of Horse also accompanied them, and rode up through the Body of the Church and Quire, until they came to the Altar, where they began their work. They rudely plucked down the Table, and broke the rail, they threw down the Organ, they broke the curiously carved work. From thence they turned to the Monuments of the Dead ; some they utterly demolished ; others they defaced. Having wreaked their fury on the beautiful chantries, they flung down several of the Mortuary chests, wherein were deposited the bones of Bishops, and scattered the bones all over the pavement of the church." [1]

This melancholy account speaks for all the vandalism of the years of the Great Rebellion, though much more was destroyed than the treasures enumerated in the chronicler's story. Fox's stained glass was smashed by pikes and the butts of muskets—and by stranger weapons ; for the troopers amused themselves by throwing the bones from the mortuary chests at the windows. The Cathedral library was twice ransacked. The priceless store of books, manuscripts and monastic records were scattered about the close to rot. Worst of all, perhaps, was the breaking of " the curiously carved work " mentioned by Bruno Ryves. The reference is undoubtedly to the series of fourteenth-century carvings of biblical scenes which stood beneath the canopies of the choir stalls. [2]

Two months before his execution, Charles I passed, a captive, through Winchester between silent crowds and the ranks of the Mayor and Corporation who, defiantly, made their final act of homage dressed in their robes of office. By then only the fabric of the Cathedral was really whole, and even that was threatened. So dreadful was the decay that in 1653 it was seriously proposed to demolish the Cathedral for want of funds to repair it. With some difficulty money was found to make the roofs watertight. The bill amounted to about forty pounds.

The story of the Cathedral during the next three centuries is one of its preservation after the years of ruin. As its walls now declare, not all the restorations and the erection of memorials were happily inspired. Some of the monuments of the broad-minded ecclesiastics of the eighteenth century are, in a refined way, aggressive acts of vandalism. The nineteenth-century " restorers ", too, were destroyers on the grand scale—though with the best of intentions. " If there exists a power to arrest such proceedings," wrote a horrified young architect in 1820, " that power ought firmly to be exercised." No power, however, could arrest the serene progress of Victorian Bad Taste. Among many examples of it the most notable is the sham-Gothic tomb of the good Bishop Wilberforce—its effect on the appearance of the south transept is ruinous.

Yet in the main the last three hundred years have preserved to us the great House of God that Walkelin built and his successors glorified. Under all the chances of time, its walls are a record, complete enough, of nine centuries of the history, the taste, the emotions, and the highest aspirations of the English folk whose hands and whose devotion went to its making.

[1] *Mercurius Rusticus*, Bruno Ryves ; 1685. Quoted in *Winchester Cathedral*, John Vaughan, M.A. ; Selwyn and Blount, 1919.
[2] See page 28.

Part II

THE TREASURES OF THE HOUSE

7 : *The Chantry Chapels*

ALL the bishops who built Winchester Cathedral lie buried within the walls which are their enduring monument. Walkelin was buried in the nave where steps led to the choir beneath the great cross of Bishop Stigand. He had no stone and no monument, and needs none. The whole Cathedral is his memorial. De Lucy lies beneath a simple marble tomb in the centre of his exquisite retrochoir. Edington and Wykeham were laid to rest in the nave which was the work of their inspiration. Fox, old and blind, prepared himself a tomb by the side of the choir to which he had added so rich a beauty. The last three of these great builders all lie within their chantry chapels, as do four more (if we include Langton's chapel in the list of chantries) of Winchester's bishops—Beaufort, Wayneflete, Langton and Gardiner. These chantries are the most splendid of the Cathedral's monuments. There are richer chantries than any of them in other English cathedrals, but no cathedral in this country has a series of chantries of such beauty as Winchester has. There is nowhere so complete a sequence of the architectural styles of the centuries in which the dying greatly feared to set out on their journey without the assurance of the prayers of the living.

Edington's chantry is the earliest of the enclosed chantries at Winchester. It is also the simplest. It lies between two of the pillars on the south of the nave where (as the Bishop directed his executors) " the monks are wont to make a station in procession on the Lord's day and festivals ". It was probably built after his death, when the tomb was surrounded by a low white stone screen of great grace and dignity. The alabaster figure of the Bishop is—for all its mutilation—the best of the tomb-sculptures in the Cathedral. Like all such figures, the pale alabaster effigy was once bright with colour and blazed with jewels. On the bands of the mitre are the sockets from which the despoilers tore the precious stones which decorated it. The symbols of the Bishop's authority, and the supporters at his head and feet have been hacked away. But the figure itself remains largely untouched—a gracious example of early Gothic artistry.

Wykeham's chantry lies four bays below that of Edington's and is from the outside far more magnificent. [It was erected during Wykeham's lifetime and was therefore built as an integral part of the reconstruction of the nave.] It occupies the whole space of one of the bays, the pinnacles of its canopy reaching to the balustrades beneath the clerestory. The design is simple but majestic. The lower part, which forms a screen to the chapel, is in three tiers of graceful panels and lights of increasing height. From them spring two high and slender pillars which, with the outer pillars of the nave itself, enclose three arches crowned with pinnacles. The effect is dramatic, as it is meant to be. But it is harmonious ; the work of a designer whose eye for effect was never allowed to master his sense of proportion.

The chantry was, of course, stripped of all its statues by the iconoclasts, but the figure was unharmed. It was saved from the axes of the Roundhead soldiers, we are told, by an Old Wykehamist, Nathaniel Fiennes, who loyally stood guard over the tomb of the founder of the College, sword in hand. The effigy is a fine one, carved with much care for detail and conveying the sense of a man in whom the possession of great authority was tempered by a humane character.

The lively figures at Wykeham's feet of three tonsured men in clerical robes have been variously identified. William Cobbett, who came riding into Winchester with his son one day in 1812, set down one of his confident mis-statements when he recorded that " Wykeham lies on his back in his catholic dress and shepherd's Crook with little children at his feet saying their prayers ". Others have suggested that the figures represent three favourite monks, or three clerics who were to say the masses for his soul, or the executors of the Bishop's will. It is far more likely (the figures are dressed in the robes of lay clerics) that they are the three master-craftsmen who were responsible for rebuilding the nave.

It is very quiet within the tiny space of the chantry. There is none of the tension of the nave here, and little of its majesty. In spite of the great height of the canopy with its intricate *lierne* vaulting and in spite of the large tomb and its almost life-sized figure, the sense is one of intimacy and utter stillness as soon as the door is closed on the nave. His hands closed in prayer, his robes richly painted in sombre colours, the Bishop lies " overthrown by death " (as the inscription on the edge of the tomb has it) but enclosed by a deep peace purged of all the terrors of mortality and beyond the need of the ceaseless prayers for which, for nearly five centuries, the chantry has asked.

The chantry built for Beaufort is of a very different kind. This is no enclosed space for withdrawal and for prayer. It is the tomb of a prince, a splendid housing for the perpetual lying-in-state of a man of great position in the world. Beneath the great arched canopy, the effigy lies high on its tomb. It is separated from the aisles of the retrochoir by low rails of Purbeck marble which serve the haughty purposes of a barrier and of a command to look upon the impressive figure of a man who was in no doubt of the splendour of his nobility and of the justice of his right to great authority.

The designer of this tomb did not merely surround it with grandeur, however; he created a monument of superbly refined artistry which, in its style, is the loveliest in this country. In detail it is subtle, sophisticated and richly worked; but its general effect is one of majestic simplicity. The design is composed of a great rounded central arch supported on each side by lesser rounded arches all so harmoniously placed that they seem as if hung in folds of a rich damask rather than carved, stone by stone, from Purbeck marble. The impression of hangings, as of a draped tent, is strengthened by the mouldings of the panels and pillars which are individually of great delicacy and, in the mass, of noble strength. The arches are crowned by an elaborate canopy of pinnacles which rise in a cluster towards the roof of the retrochoir like the towers of an ancient city upon a hilltop to the sky. They are obviously the work of restorers. In the early nineteenth century the settlement of the floor in this part of the Cathedral tore the canopy apart, and the original marble pinnacles fell down.

As the chantry was built to glorify the Cardinal from without rather than to provide a place of retreat and prayer within, the interior restates the theme of princeliness. The vaulting of the canopy is of great beauty, and its tracery seeks to lead the eye to a central angel who holds, naturally enough, Beaufort's proud arms : *France quartered with England*. On the sides of the tomb are painted shields with the devices of the Garter, the cardinal's hat, the mitre, and Beaufort's own arms and those of his see. The figure of the Cardinal himself is a crude piece of mason's work which was added in the late seventeenth century, and is of no merit whatsoever except that for want of a better effigy it preserves complete the original design of the tomb.

There is no inscription on the tomb, no record in words of the life of the man to which it is raised. Yet there did exist, at the beginning of the seventeenth century we are told, a fragment of brass which had escaped the attention of the destroyers. It read : *Tribularer si nescirem misericordias tuas*—I should be in anguish if I did not know Thy mercies. The cry is the more moving for the strange contrast provided by its proud and confident setting. It is difficult to understand the motives of the living ; there is no unlocking the secrets of the minds and hearts of the dead. To Beaufort, perhaps, most aptly applies the epigram of Anatole France: " *La miséricorde de Dieu est infinie; elle sauvera même un riche* ".

Wayneflete's chantry stands close to that of Beaufort and is built to the same majestic design of arched screens supporting a pinnacled canopy. Comparison is inevitable, but is a task better abandoned, since nice distinctions between equal beauties add little to the understanding. The chantries are indeed strikingly similar, but the differences between them are sufficiently wide for the one to be of quite different character from the other. Where the earlier tomb is cut from soft-textured, grey-brown Purbeck marble, the later is of dazzling white stone. The decoration of one is simple, reticent ; of the other, elaborate and fanciful. Beaufort's central arch is opened wide like the proscenium of a theatre. Wayneflete's is screened, enclosing the effigy within its private place. Both are sumptuous, but only one sets out to be dramatic.

As usual the figures which stood in the niches inside and outside the chantry have gone. But there remain the delightful carvings on the niches themselves. Among them can be seen a tiny pair of wrestlers hugely enjoying themselves, and an angry lawyer wrestling with a furious monk over a book. The detail inside the chantry is also of great delicacy. In the centre of the fan-vaulted roof an angel shows the Bishop's coat of arms to the upturned face of the effigy on the tomb beneath—an effect which is without drama or significance, for the gorgeously painted effigy is as lifeless as was the inspiration of the craftsman who carved it. Looking at the heart which the bishop holds between his hands, a too-literal interpretation of the liturgical *sursum corda*, one reflects that it was not only the restorers of our ancient cathedrals who were liable to error in matters of taste.

Though Stephen Gardiner's was the last built of Winchester's chantries, that of Richard Fox is the crown of the series and in some respects the loveliest of them all, for it is without blemish. It takes the form of a screen-enclosed chapel built between two of de Lucy's pillars in the south aisle of the retrochoir. Its combination of the utmost refinement of detail with the grace of its proportions produces an effect in which strength and delicacy are exquisitely balanced. Little of the white stone is undecorated. Apart from the profusion of other details, there are no fewer than fifty-five niches on the outside of the chantry—all with elaborately carved pedestals and groined canopies. The lowest tier is carved with slender pilasters supporting fourteen figures (alas, they are modern substitutes) each about two feet high. Above them hang tiny canopies whose vaults are all of different design. This tier is separated from those above it by a foliated frieze of supreme workmanship. The pattern of small leaves is so cut and pierced from the solid stone that no substance is left, and only a skein of lace-like foliage remains. Above it rise three-tiered windows (once said to contain stained glass) of Renaissance design into which are successfully woven four sets of double Gothic ogee arches. On the top of the screen is another magnificently carved frieze from which spring a series of pinnacles. On each alternate one perches Fox's device of the pelican in her piety.

All this rich detail is carved with a loving and exquisite hand. The finials of the miniature clusters of pinnacles which break the five main pillars of the south face of the chantry are, for instance, wonderfully carved in the shape of animals and birds—eagles, bears, bats and monkeys. They are not noticeable unless the carving is examined very closely. None of them is more than an inch and a half long. The exuberance which went to their invention was under the discipline of a master-artist who saw the work constantly as a whole.

There is no tombstone inside the chantry, which is a true chapel with an altar and, behind it, a tiny vestry. Like the exterior, it is richly carved with many niches for the figures of the saints. Above the altar is a series of coats of arms which, like those on Fox's presbytery vault, are emblazoned with symbols of the Passion. The chantry is a monument to Fox's own taste, for it was built early during his long episcopacy, and he used it frequently for private prayer. When, towards the end of his long life, he became infirm and blind, he used to be led into it to remain there for many hours together. He was fortunate in the date of his death. When he was buried beneath the floor of his chantry on October 5, 1528, the dissolution of the monasteries was only seven years ahead, and the grievous destruction of the Cathedral's treasures, for whose provision he had himself so devotedly laboured, was to follow four years after.

Into the face of the splendid screen of the chantry which faces the aisle of the retrochoir, and almost at ground level, a recess is built in the shape of a tomb. Within it lies the carving of a parched and wasted corpse, its head upon a mitre, its feet against a skull. It is a gesture of humility and admonition not without pride. "This is what I am", says Fox's grim cadaver. "This is what I was", reply the walls of the chantry. We can hardly doubt which of the two messages Fox, the humanist, a man devoted to the touch and shape and colour of all things lovely, preferred us to remember.

There is one more chantry in the Cathedral. It lies opposite to that of Fox, and was built for the reception of the remains of Gardiner. It is ill-proportioned journeyman's work : a botching together of styles as unsuitable to each other as Gothic, Ionic Greek, and Renaissance, and none of it good of its kind. This unconvincing structure is a confession of failure, as if its walls were built to symbolize a life which was always a bitter struggle and which ended in defeat. The Old Faith was doomed, its symbols and ceremonies were passing out of use, and this—the last expression in stone that the Cathedral possesses of the beliefs of pre-Reformation times—was built too late to be warmed even by a spark of the inspiration which had so splendidly expressed itself in the stones of Winchester Cathedral for the past five centuries.

Within the chantry, the tale is also one of desolation. The floor is bare. In one corner there is exposed the stump of one of the pillars of the original Norman arch. The altar is gone. Above its place there is a representation in relief of a Greek temple. At first sight it appears merely incongruous, perhaps ridiculous. But then one realizes how apt a record it is of its time. What else could better serve as an altar decoration in days which had violently broken from the past, but had not yet found new forms of expression, than a non-controversial symbol of an alien belief that was very, very dead ?

8 : *Chapels and Wall Paintings*

DURING the long history of the English cathedrals the enclosure of parts of their structure as chapels set apart from the main body of the church was undertaken for a variety of reasons. From the earliest days, and especially in those times when English folk were wont "to goon on pilgrimages", aisles and transepts were filled with chapels or shrines at which the pilgrim could pray before the relic of a saint. Chapels were also dedicated to celebrations of the great festivals of the Christian year. Later, with the increasing importance in monastic ritual of the worship of the Virgin Mary, Lady Chapels were set aside or—more frequently— built on to the cathedral walls. After the time of the Black Death, as we have seen, bishops and other great dignitaries of the church either built themselves enclosed chantries, or screened off an already existing chapel in which masses could be perpetually offered for the peace of their souls.   Noble families, too, were apt to appropriate to themselves corners of the cathedrals : and so also—especially in the eighteenth century—were the deans, prebendaries or canons of the cathedrals and their numerous families.   The tradition—and it is a fitting one—of providing within a necessarily public and busy building a private space for prayer is still maintained.   There are few cathedrals which do not preserve at least one of these quiet retreats for those who come to worship.

Winchester's chapels provide examples of nearly all the reasons for enclosure of the aisles.   Between them they house some of the Cathedral's most precious treasures ; especially, they contain three sets of splendid wall paintings—all that is left to us as a reminder that once the walls and roofs were everywhere rich with paint.   Colour did not adorn the walls only for its own sake.   There was a very reasonable motive for the huge frescoes which looked down on the congregations in the public parts of the medieval cathedrals.

" The peasant as he stood or knelt on the floor of the Church each Sunday " (says G. M. Trevelyan) " could not follow the Latin words, but good thoughts found a way into his heart as he watched what he revered and heard the familiar yet still mysterious sounds.   Around him blazed on the walls frescoes of scenes from the scriptures and the lives of saints ; and over the roodloft was the Last Judgment depicted in lively colours, paradise opening to receive the just, and on the other side flaming hell with devil executioners tormenting naked souls." [1]

Time, the depredations of iconoclasts and the freakish tastes of restorers have stripped cathedral walls of saints and sinners, paradises and hells.   Often, indeed, it is because restorers covered up offending frescoes with coats of plaster or powder-wash that they have survived at all.

The most ancient of Winchester's wall paintings are to be found in its oldest chapel— the Chapel of the Holy Sepulchre in the north transept.   The chapel lies on the south side of the transept between two of the enormous Norman pillars which support the central tower.   Even at first sight, before anything is known of its story, it strangely troubles the emotions.   It is so very small a place to lie beneath so grandiose an arch.   It has been much rebuilt by many hands, most recently when the organ was installed above it.   But the marvel is that in spite of all the patchings it has undergone its essential character is retained.   It looks rough-hewn, untidy ; as if cut out from the natural rock.   There is an air of solemnity and secrecy about it.   Like no other part of the Cathedral, it is unorganized and refreshingly free of the graces of form and style.

This was once a most holy place. Possibly it was used only once in the year in the Good Friday and Easter Day ceremonies.   Certainly it was a shrine which faced all pilgrims to the tomb of Saint Swithun as they entered the Cathedral, and was an object of their special devotion.

In its present form its exterior consists of two bays with two rough arches of Early English style.   The bay on the left is railed to reveal, dimly, a small altar.   The other bay is walled for most of its height by a screen pierced only by an entry door and a simply carved quatrefoil.   It has been said that through this small " window " the arms of generations of pilgrims reached to seek an access of virtue or healing from contact with so holy a place.   The stone on the lower part of the quatrefoil is worn quite smooth.

Inside the chapel the sense of a sepulchre hewn from the face of a rock increases.   Even the accidents of time and the hasty work of rebuilders have all helped to sustain the impression.   Or perhaps the character of this tiny space was too dominant for the botchers ever to extinguish it.   All the walls and vaults and the floor (paved with old gravestones)

[1] *English Social History*, G. M. Trevelyan, O.M.   Longmans, Green & Co., London, 1942.

are rough in texture. The Norman piers at the west end are broken off. One vault has been destroyed and the stones of the rear wall are exposed. Very little daylight enters. Here, there is the dimness, the narrowness, and the mystery of the Tomb.

Yet all these walls were once vivid with colour. The paintings that remain on the chapel's east bay are faded and broken. Only an expert in medieval paintings (these are of the early thirteenth century) will have great pleasure in them. But the patient visitor will see one striking panel and will, if he allows his imagination to respond to the magic of this little place, be able to re-create much of the ancient beauty of these walls.

The one splendid remnant is that which occupies the chapel's east vault and the wall beneath it. A huge head and shoulders of Christ fills the triangle of the vault. It is drawn in bold, pure lines of black and chrome, blue and red. The effect of this masterly drawing is one of serenity and majesty. It commands the entire chapel. Immediately beneath this figure is a Deposition and below that—though it is much faded —the scene of the Burial in the Tomb. There is a dramatic agony of movement in these figures whose faces emerge from the faded walls with extraordinary force and energy. Those who examine the grieving face of Mary or the face of the dead Christ, deeply marked with anguish yet utterly drained of will, of spirit, and of life, will know that they stand before a work of genius.

There is one other chapel in the north transept. In its present state the Epiphany Chapel (as it is called) is of modern making, and is bounded by a screen enclosing the entire west aisle of the transept. The chapel is now set aside as a place for private prayer, and contains windows designed by Burne-Jones which (though the reds of the glass are poor) are striking for the colour and handling of the olive-green foliage. The chapel almost certainly continues a tradition of enclosure that goes back to Norman times. For this aisle stood at the door through which the pilgrims made their entry, and was probably once a vestibule and a space for the storage of the pilgrims' gifts to the Cathedral. It contains a number of heads of kings and bishops carved with considerable vigour—and apparently at random—in the pillars and on the walls. They are not capitals. They support nothing. They are so unexpected, indeed, that one is forced to such fanciful conclusions as that either a stonemason chose to exercise his skill here in preparation for more serious tasks, or that the carver thought the severe walls needed enlivening and so scattered his heads where his fancy led him to set his chisel to work.

The three chapels at the east end of the Cathedral were built in the thirteenth century when the Norman apse was taken down and replaced by de Lucy's gracious retrochoir, and all three, perhaps, were devoted to the worship of the Virigin Mary. The central chapel is still known as the Lady Chapel. Those on either side of it were later enclosed as chantries for two of Winchester's bishops. The south chapel is still known as Langton's Chapel. (Langton held the see from 1493-1500.) The north chapel has been described on doubtful authority as the chapel of Bishop Orlton, a little-known fourteenth-century prelate. It is now more happily known by the lovely name of the Chapel of the Guardian Angels from the marvellous frescoes which decorate the vault.

This painted roof is of special value because, through careful restoration, it enables us to judge how the Cathedral looked when its walls and vaults were bright with colour. The four divisions of the vault and the ribs that support them are all decorated ; the ribs with a simple ripple pattern in ochres, shades of red and black, the vaults with an elaborate pattern of foliage and azure stars among which hang, brilliant as major stars, the medallions of winged angels. They are of thirteenth-century workmanship, drawn with the self-confidence which belongs only to those days when the world seems young and men are too occupied in the joys of making and creating to bedevil their work by theorizing about it.

The paintings are bright with happiness and gay with worship. They are the legacies of a time when gaiety was no exile from the observances and rituals of the Christian faith.

Langton's Chapel on the south is a perfect example of the enclosure of an existing chapel as the chantry of a dead prelate. The enclosure was achieved by throwing a wooden screen across the entry and by dressing the inner walls with elaborately carved wood panelling whose overhanging canopies have the effect of creating a second roof below the chapel's vault, and of narrowing the chapel into a private housing for the large and simple tomb of the Bishop.

Like Wayneflete, Langton was an educator and a lover of the humanities. If we knew nothing more of him, we should love him a little for his joy in music and for his remark addressed to those who have the duty of civilizing small boys (his habit was to take his scholars through their grammar in the evenings) : " The way to increase virtue is to praise it."

He was Provost of Queen's College, Oxford, before becoming Bishop of Salisbury, was translated to Winchester in 1493, and was appointed Archbishop of Canterbury a few days before his death in 1500. He was never installed as Archbishop—a fact which did not prevent those who decorated his chantry from carving a shield which shows his own arms impaled with those of Canterbury. In the exquisite tracing of the chapel's vault, punning rebuses typical of the times can be seen. Langton's name is represented by a " long " (a note in old musical notation) on a tun, that of Prior Hunton, by a hen—also carved upon a barrel.

In addition to its architectural beauties the Lady Chapel also contains some fine but much mutilated woodwork and a set of delightful late fifteenth-century wall paintings. All that needs to be said about the aesthetic value of these paintings is that they are the work of a competent draughtsman and a skilled technician. Their virtue lies in the vigour with which they adorn a tale and point a moral. Like many painters of the Victorian age, this artist was required to tell a story in pictures. His theme was that of the miraculous loving-kindness of the Virgin Mary, and he illustrated it by painting a series of panels based on popular tales and legends of the day. There are twenty-two of them, and two more panels over the doors on each side of the chapel—one of which represents the Annunciation, and the other Prior Silkstede kneeling before a figure of Mary. Beneath his picture is a scroll which reads : " Prior Silkstede caused these polished stones, O Mary, to be decorated at his own expense."

The pictures are laid out in two rows on the north and south walls of the chapel. They are divided vertically by naturalistically painted pillars, and horizontally by flat canopies coloured to represent stone and carrying brief descriptions of the episodes illustrated above them. The artist's purpose (it is one which betrays the hand of a technician rather than of an artist) was, in fact, to create an illusion of figures carved into stone recesses. Therefore he did not—as was customary with medieval artists—use a set of brilliant colours. He worked in black and white with only rare touches of green and red—except where he had to draw a pair of flying devils which, by ancient tradition, required their unmistakable habit of black and blue and red.

Visitors will have their own preferences among the episodes whose stories are so plainly set forth that they hardly need the help of a guide to explain their significance. There is a picture of a painter from whose feet a winged, malicious devil has whipped a ladder because, the story tells, the painter had taken gross liberties with his (the devil's) portrait. The painter hangs in mid-air above the porch of a church clutching the hand of a statue of the Madonna which had stretched out its arm to save the painter from hurt. In another, a hangman is in the act of tying a blindfolded rogue by the neck to the gallows. But the thief had never omitted to make his prayers to the Virgin who, having pity on him

for his devotion, is shown kneeling to support the weight of his feet. A third shows an executioner attempting to strike off the hand of Saint John Damascene, accused of heresies. Through the Virgin's intervention the hand remains miraculously upon the wrist of the wrongfully accused man.

The originals of all these paintings—some of them seriously faded—remain on the chapel walls. But what the visitor first sees are hinged panels upon which Professor E. W. Tristram has wonderfully copied and reconstructed the episodes that lie behind them. Those who wish to see what is left of these records of the improving legends of the late medieval ages have only to swing the copies back on the hinges—and be grateful for the understanding lent them by Professor Tristram's loving craftsmanship.

There remain two more enclosed chapels in the Cathedral, each of which occupies a bay of the east aisle of the south transept.

How the Venerable Chapel came by its name is not known, nor do we know for what purpose the chapel was enclosed. The title may be old; it may be the inspiration of a canon or a servant of the church who loved it, perhaps, for the glorious screen which covers the whole of the Norman arch. The screen is apt to be overlooked, for the Cathedral contains so many treasures which are more obvious. It should not be passed lightly, however, because no stonework in the Cathedral is more lovely. Antiquarians have attributed it to various dates in the fourteenth or fifteenth centuries. It is therefore safest to say that its style is that of the early Gothic craftsmen: a white stone screen composed of two tiers of windows from which springs a canopy composed of seven slender pinnacles supported on shafts. Its beauty lies in the perfect balance of the strength and severity of its lines, and the delicacy of its proportions.

During the eighteenth century the chapel became almost the private vault of members of the Eyre family one of whom was responsible for the lovely iron screen at the chapel's entrance. Ten dignified memorial tablets to the Eyres hang on the chapel walls. Their reticence and dignity does something to restore confidence in the good taste of an age which, if it did not pride itself on its religious enthusiasm, certainly considered itself incapable of breaches of a refined standard of aesthetic sensibility. Elsewhere in the Cathedral its memorials are not so happy.

The second of the south transept chapels occupies the bay next to the Venerable Chapel, and is named after Prior Silkstede, Fox's partner in the work of glorifying the Cathedral up to the days of the Reformation. Silkstede's Christian name, Thomas, is borne on shields on the cornice of the screen. Whether or not this was once the Prior's chantry chapel, it is not to pray for the repose of this good man's soul that many people now make the journey to visit this corner of Winchester Cathedral. For beneath a stone in the floor of the chapel lies Izaak Walton, gentlest of men, sweetest of writers, and most ardent of fishermen. He lived the last contented years of a contented life in Winchester, much occupied—as the indifferent twentieth-century glass window shows—in fishing the Itchen not far from the Cathedral.

He would have liked the verse that was composed for his tomb. It reads:

Alas! Hee's gone before,
Gone, to return no more,
Our panting Breasts aspire
After their aged Sire,
Whose well-spent life did last
Full ninety Years, and past.
But now he hath begun
That which will nere be done,
Crown'd with eternal Blisse
We wish our Souls with his.

It is not good verse—even for a bishop. (Bishop Ken is said to have been the author.) But it would have delighted Walton, a constant lover of simple things and innocent pleasures. He was not the man to have desired to lie at last beneath the grievous burden of a lengthy obituary notice inscribed in Latin.

9 : *The Art of the Wood-Carver*

IN the summer of 1635 a Lieutenant of the Military Company stationed in Norwich was looking forward to his leave. His plans were precise and they were elaborate, but they were not those customary to Army officers temporarily liberated from the irksome duties of arms drill and barrack-room inspections. This was a most unusual Lieutenant. He was an enthusiastic traveller, an amateur antiquary, and the diligent compiler of a travel diary. The year before he had passed a delightful leave touring northern England on horseback and had covered twelve hundred miles. Now he planned to repeat this delectable experience and to see what antiquities in the south-west of England might be worthy of description in his diary.

So, in the company of a Captain and an Ancient[1] he rode one day into Winchester, where the marvels of the Cathedral dazzled his eyes and set his pen busily to work in the pages of his diary. He was specially enthusiastic about the carvings which stood behind the canopies of the choir stalls. " And as above on the Roofe " (the Lieutenant wrote) " so over the Deanes, Prebends, and Quiristers seats, is rich Joyners worke ; but more remark'ble, in artificiall and rare Postures, ravishing the eyes of the beholders is a lively, wooddy, Representation, Portraiets, and Images, from the Creation, to the Passion, W^ch though it tooke me some time to take, yet I thought it neverthelesse not idely, ill spent time for me to decipher the same, as I found it, and heere to insert it."

The Lieutenant then wrote out (and it was fortunate indeed that he did so) a full list of these " ravishing representations ". Among them he saw, for instance, a sequence on the north side of the stalls :

" Noah warn'd by God to build an Arke."
" The Arke is built and the creatures pr'serv'd."
" Noah is drunke, and his 3 Sons described."

Elsewhere he noted a scene which depicted " Ezekiah on his death bed ; hath 15 yeeres added." In another, " John preaching in the Wilderness to the people, the ffowles and Beasts listning to him."[2] In all the diarist described sixty-one carvings. Those on the north side were scenes from the Old Testament ; those on the south from the New, and divided between scenes of Christ's childhood and his Passion. It was a providential visit for us, who know of these " lively, wooddy, Images " only because of the Lieutenant's enthusiasm for antiquities. He was only just in time. Eight years later Waller's Puritan soldiers chopped and hacked them all away. The shelf on which they stood is empty, its walls now painted blue and powdered with golden stars.

Fortunately the zeal of the Roundhead pikemen did not urge them to destroy the choir stalls. For this much we can be grateful, for Winchester's stalls are not only the oldest in England that have remained to us almost intact, but are also, perhaps, the most lovely of their time in any English church or cathedral.

Most unusually we do not have to guess at the period of their construction, for we know the name of the craftsman who designed them and the date at which they were

[1] The rank that Pistol held. The word was a corruption of Ensign.
[2] The full list of these carvings is reprinted in *Winchester Cathedral Record* No. 4, 1943.

built. A letter exists written in 1308 by Bishop Woodlock to the Bishop of Norwich asking him to lend the carpenter William Lyngwode to Winchester until such time as the stalls were completed. The task was finished in seven years. The stalls are disposed around the sides of the choir in the normal fashion with twenty-six seats on the north and south sides and ten return stalls at the west end. They were, of course, for the use of the brethren of St. Swithun's Priory who were sixty when their numbers were at full strength.

William Lyngwode was, as the work reveals, a craftsman of genius whose creative joy was in the decoration rather than in the general design of his work. For the plan of his stalls he simply used that which was the architectural currency of his day : the pinnacles and canopies developed by the stonemasons and therefore, if we are to be scrupulous, not best suited to a craftsman in wood. The design is thus composed of a series of seats behind which is placed a screen decorated with the pointed arch and foliated spandrels. Above the seats hang the spired canopies, divided by pinnacles. Within each canopy the main arch encloses a foliated medallion which is supported on two sub-arches divided by a plain and slender pillar. The oak from which they were made is almost black with age, sombre and rich and of magnificent dignity. It is difficult to realize that, as the Cathedral walls were once a blaze of colour, so this lovely oak glowed with gold-leaf and the clear, bright paints of the medieval palette.

You may spend hours together in these marvellous stalls and not exhaust your wonder at the lavishness of their decoration and the grace and high spirits of their details. They have been carved with such generosity and so rich a spending of happiness at the feel of the chisel as it created loveliness from the baulks and planks of timber as they lay on the bench. It is as though the carvers could not contain the exuberance of their fancy. Innocent-looking cusps suddenly reveal tiny, grinning heads. Formal-seeming pinnacles flower with a startling crop of lion-like masks. A vigorous portrait head detaches itself from the junction of two canopies. Everywhere richly carved foliage contains a bestiary born out of the lively imagination of stay-at-homes who listened to the handsome yarns of travellers returned from lands upon the world's edge. Yet all this richness is severely confined within the formal design of the whole. It is nowhere permitted to draw attention to itself. It observes the most perfect of architectural good manners—which explains why many visitors are apt to miss the half of its beauties.

The most accessible of the details are the carvings in the spandrels above the arches of the wall screen. All are filled with foliage of a pattern neither realistic nor wholly conventional. At least six varieties of leaf can be identified, some of them obviously based on the oak, the vine and the ivy. In many of the spandrels the foliage contains unexpected portraits in "rare postures". A sad monkey plucks listlessly on a harp. A dragon, bearded and winged, grins as he balances himself upon his nose. Another, and more cheerful, monkey scratches his chest in a tree, and a horse tramples a boar underfoot. There is a vigorous portrait of a falconer in stiff peaked cap carrying a falcon on his heavily gloved wrist. There is a knight in surcoat and head armour of chain-mail who waves a broadsword and a round shield. Another swordsman—like a fearsomely decorated devil-dancer from the other side of the world—sprouts a spread of foliage from each corner of his mouth. There is the ancient complaint against the monstrous regiment of women in the carving of a dragon whose head is unmistakably that of a woman wearing the mouth-veil, or yashmak.

The other details on the canopies and their supporting pillars all reward a close examination. There is the fine series of heads carved beneath the joints of the canopies. All of them were probably portrait heads of monks or of cathedral craftsmen. There are the exquisitely carved foliate piercings—all of different design—enclosed by the inner arches of the canopies. There are the tiny heads that have been carved into the points of the four cusps of the arches above each of the seats. And there are, too, hidden away out of sight the carvings of the misericords.

It is always a pity to spoil a satisfying story; but it is not the truth that these narrow seats were designed with the harsh purpose of throwing sleepy monks to the floor if they foolishly began to doze during the services. Their object, as the name implies, was indeed a humane one. They were designed (much as is the modern shooting-stick) to allow weary monks to lean on them during the frequent and often long devotions of the Bene-dictine Rule.

The craftsmen who made them decorated these hidden misericords with the same love and exuberance that they gave to details that were exposed to the light of day. Those at Winchester appear to be by a cruder hand than that which carved the stalls. But they are full of life, of observation of simple, homely things, and of the freakish or impish fancies of the medieval craftsmen. All the misericords have three carvings : a medallion at each ear of the rest, and a boss beneath. They range from simple patterns of foliage, to human heads, angels playing musical instruments, devils, and illustrations of popular legends and folklore. Among them are also several carvings of domestic animals : a cat caught at the moment in which it lifts a captured mouse in its teeth and makes a rapid survey of the ground for a secret place in which to devour it ; a chick clumsily, but with enormous pleasure, making its first attempts at flapping its wings ; an indifferently blissful sow suckling her young. They are carvings which wonderfully preserve for us the temper and mind and humours of these long-dead craftsmen, and of the very English jests that relieved the tedium of the day's labour in the workshop. One carver, for instance, made his comment on some superior who had irritated him by cutting a bust of a craftsman who holds a chisel in his hand and pokes a scornful tongue at foremen, bosses, patrons, and the whole tribe of those set in authority over him. Another, carving the portrait head of a woman, rid himself doubtless of a heavy burden of domestic grievance by cutting delicately away behind the lips until he had set free a wooden tongue which has wagged every time the seat has been moved for six centuries, and will, presumably, continue to wag so long as there are men and women left to involve themselves in the skirmishes of married life.

The sub-stalls which line the choir were built during the last years of the reign of Henry VIII and are of special interest as the only constructive memorials the Cathedral possesses of a period otherwise given to the melancholy activities of destruction. The backs of these stalls contain a number of beautifully carved panels of Renaissance design. Probably they were the work of Italian craftsmen ; certainly there is a Roman firmness and spaciousness in their shaping. Among them are a panel dated 1540, the royal arms with Henry's cipher, a Tudor rose, and the arms of Stephen Gardiner and William Kings-mill, last of the Priors of St. Swithun's. Most interesting of them all is the panel carved with the arms that were granted to the new Dean and Chapter in 1541. They were drawn up, says the proclamation of the Garter King of Arms, as a reward for the " honorable Demeanour and vertuouse governance of the ryght Worshypfull Deans and Chanons ". The arms show a pair of plump cherubs supporting a shield which carries the device of a church of Saxon design. In its gate is a curious figure representing the Blessed Trinity. In the top left-hand corner of the shield is the Tudor rose dressed, like the midday sun, with a crown of rays of light.

Scarcely less magnificent than the woodwork in the choir is that of two of the east chapels, Langton's and the Lady Chapel. The screens in Langton's chapel have already been briefly described. They are of extraordinary richness and, though deriving from the forms invented by the stonemasons, are worked in details that are appropriate only to the wood from which they are carved. They show the theme of the Gothic arch decorated to the highest degree of elaboration it is capable of sustaining without becoming overloaded and a mere jumble of arabesques.

The woodwork of the Lady Chapel is of a very different kind. The screen is of a simple late Decorated style and, by the side of the riches of the carving in Langton's Chapel, looks at first rather meagre—as do the stalls and their canopies which line the Early English half of the chapel. This woodwork has in fact been most grievously mutilated. It is the saddest of losses, for what is left of it shows, as only three or four remarkable stone fragments elsewhere in the Cathedral show to the same degree, the warmth and the vitality of the Old Faith. The carvings left on the stalls and bench-ends of this chapel are of meticulous realism. They are the products of a faith strong enough to laugh at its own follies, and tender enough to remember that the mouse and the sparrow were also among the glories of God's creation. They speak of a time that was not too old to have lost the instant freshness of vision which could make poetry out of the most common or most mean of objects, nor yet too young to have missed the revivifying warmth of the new spirit of the humanists of the Renaissance.

Is this too large a claim for a few small fragments of carved wood? If it is, the charm at least of the figures in the Lady Chapel is irresistible. The best of them are to be found in the finials of the bench-ends. On the right of the entrance is a pair of those tumblers, familiar to every medieval teller-of-tales, who danced their hearts out for the pleasure of the Lady Mary. These tumblers lean back to grasp their calves in an ecstasy of effort no less intense for the fact that their positions are dictated by the curve of the finials. The shirt of one of them gapes from the string of his trousers. The woollen ribbing of a pair of trousers and a tear in a pair of hose are lovingly carved into the wood. Opposite the tumblers the wings of another finial enclose a small hen sitting on her wicker basket of eggs ; a mouse which scampers by, its tail waving across its back ; a swan ; and a hare. At the other end of this bench are two enchanting figures of sturdy beggars. Each bows low—an ingratiating and practised bending of the back—and holds his cap in hand. One, however, strokes his beard and scowls with the outraged air of a man whose best efforts have been wasted upon a passer-by with a black soul and a heart of granite. His cap is empty. The second positively leers with professional politeness and exudes an air of false bonhomie as an over-ripe plum drips juice. In his cap lie two fat coins.

On another finial a pair of winged dragons snarl at one another their perpetual and unconsummated hatred. Elsewhere there is a pair of dolorous monkeys clinging to the post of the finial as, surely, a pair of the monks' pets—exiles from the sun—clung shivering in misery to their chain-posts in the cold, damp air of an English winter.

All the arm-rests of the stalls which once lined the chapel walls were similarly carved. All but four have either been destroyed or stolen. There are left the exquisite figures of a dog, a squirrel pouncing on a nut, and a sleeping dove. The fourth figure is a lovely thing. At first sight it shows the abandoned figure of a booted youth sprawling face downward on the earth. His long hair streams over his forehead, his legs are hooked and taut—one would say—in a terrible agony of despair. Indeed the youth's plight is desperate, but not beyond curing. He is a choir-boy temporarily overwhelmed in his struggle to free his ears from his surplice.

The latest example of pre-Reformation woodwork in the Cathedral is the splendid pulpit installed in the choir by Prior Silkstede. It is very richly carved—a superb piece of craftsmanship. Not only is Silkstede's name carved on it, but a punning reference to his name is also worked into the design of the panelling in the form of skeins of silk. This is almost the last worthy piece of the woodcarver's art with which the Cathedral was embellished. Four large and amateurish figures of the Stuart monarchs were carved as corbels to the vault beneath the tower and may now be seen in a dusty corner of the triforium gallery of the south transept.   The panels of the rails before the high altar are excellent examples of Jacobean craftsmanship, which bloom with garlands of magnificently carved flowers and the plump heads of cherubs.   But, like nearly all of the treasures of the Cathedral, most of the woodcarvings of Winchester are a legacy to us from the Age of Faith.   When that died, and with it the patronage of the great princes of the church, the doors of the cloister workshops were closed.   The craftsmen had found a new race of patrons.   They were the civil servants, the merchants, the noblemen and the adventurers whose great houses began to rise on land that for years had belonged to the monasteries and some at least of whose wealth had enriched the store of the treasures of the English cathedrals.

10 : *The Art of the Stone-Carver*

READERS of the novels of H. G. Wells may remember that when Mr. Polly was over-whelmed by the dreariness of his job in a Canterbury draper's emporium, he used to take refuge in the Cathedral and meditate in the nave.   " In the middle ages he would, no doubt," wrote Mr. Polly's creator, " have sat upon a scaffolding and carved out pene-trating and none too flattering portraits of church dignitaries upon the capitals."

The point is well made.   We should sadly misinterpret the minds of the medieval cathedral builders—laymen or clerics—if we thought of them as approaching their work in a spirit of subdued reverence or formal piety : as if the House of God were a place only for hushed whispers and a discreet shuffling of feet.   Not a bit of it.   Laughter or an uproarious pun or a sly dig at a haughty prelate were as welcome within the cathedral walls as without.   Some of our notions of what constitutes irreverence would have sadly puzzled the men of the middle ages.

The stone-carvers of Winchester have left, among much that is of abiding loveliness, ample evidence of the gaiety with which they tackled their work.   In the bosses of the vaults of nave and aisles and the decorations on the string courses beneath the nave balconies, you may find much heraldry, conventional bunches of foliage and religious symbolism.   You will also find among them such lively carvings as the portrait of two monks studying a book, and between them the cowled head of an ass reading the pages with equal seriousness ; a man setting his dog to bait a bull ; a pig astray in a vineyard ; a portrait head of a man cupping his ear and frowning desperately in his effort to hear what is being said ; and, of course, numerous freakish imps and devils, tucked away in odd corners of the vaulting.

But it is impossible to study here the generous variety of the Winchester nave and aisle bosses, or to describe all the treasures in stone that are to be found within the Cathedral walls.   A study of five examples of the stone-carver's art—one of them of great proportions, the others fragments that survived the attentions of the iconoclasts—may speak for all the stones of a Cathedral which was so splendidly decorated by its craftsmen during five centuries.

The major work is the huge stone reredos which encloses the presbytery at its east end.   It is perhaps tedious to repeat (what is the opinion of many experts) that this is the finest of its kind in any English cathedral.   What is important is the perfection of its placing and the wondrous effect of its details within the place for which it was designed. The screen was probably begun towards the end of the fifteenth century, and of its purposes two were utilitarian—to provide a strengthening bridge of stone to knit the walls of the presbytery together, and to mask the choir completely from the crowds which pressed around Saint Swithun's tomb. Its third purpose, of course, was that of glorifying the high altar.

For all the richness of its detail, the plan of the screen is simple. It consists of a wide, tall central panel which is occupied, above middle height, by a great crucifix. On each side of the panel are three tiers of canopied figures of different depths having the effect of elaborately carved pilasters. Above the screen is a rich border of ornamented stone. All the horizontal levels are so placed that the eye continually returns to the central figure on the Cross. It is this basic simplicity of design which controls the extraordinary richness of the details of the great screen. All the figures that are placed on either side of the central panel stand on elaborately carved pedestals and under pinnacled canopies of great delicacy. The border which crowns the screen is of such refined carving that it appears to have been spun from fine thread rather than carved from stone. Indeed the marvel of this reredos is that, enormous as it is, it appears to hang between the presbytery walls as lightly as would a web of lace that a breath might stir or a wind shatter. It is of dazzling white stone now ; a stone of great softness of texture which no one would wish to see covered, as once it was, with bright colours. You may still see some traces of the old medieval colouring in the spandrels above the doors which pierce the screen on either side.

These spandrels are worth examination for other reasons, too. Like all the " idolatrous images " in the Cathedral, those on the reredos were torn down in the days of the Reformation. The figures which now discreetly fill the vacant niches are of modern making. But the destroyers overlooked the small figures hidden away in the spandrels. A strange omission, for they are carvings of the Virgin Mary whose statues were elsewhere ruthlessly attacked by the iconoclasts. The spandrels show the Annunciation of the Angel to Mary, and the Visitation. They are not carvings remarkable for their artistry, though they are enchantingly fresh and vigorously made ; but they *are* remarkable for their survival. They are the only carvings of the Virgin that remain in the Cathedral in the places for which the stoneworkers designed them.

The breaking of the stone carvings at the Reformation was a catastrophe. In a few years of plunder and destruction the figured sculpture of five centuries virtually disappeared from England, and it is we who are immeasurably the poorer for this tragic loss. How great that loss is we can begin to understand a little when we study four fragments which have somehow survived the vicissitudes of time—have escaped the road-mender's hammer, the wall-builder's chisel, and the stone-crusher's ram. They are : two busts of the Madonna, one in the gallery of the triforium of the south transept, the other in the presbytery ; a head of the Almighty in the library ; and the headless figure of the Synagogue which stands framed in one of de Lucy's exquisite arcaded panels to the south of Langton's Chapel.

Those who look for these fragments will do well to begin with the little Madonna in the triforium where she is in the company of a sad collection of broken heads and limbs and bodies that once made lovely the Cathedral walls. Only the half of the figure is left, and even this has lost its arms and the crown which ringed its head. Fortunately the damage is otherwise merciful. The carving of the figure and of the cloak which is fastened below the neck by a rosette clasp and falls away over the arms to reveal a simple tunic gathered at the waist by a belt, is simply, even conventionally done : sound workshop carving, but of a good period.

There is nothing conventional, however, about the modelling of the face or the rapture with which the artist created his work. You see here a child : a child whose rounded face is unlined by the years, whose eyes look modestly down behind half-closed eyelids, and whose lips tremble with the promise of laughter. Yet this is a child whose face speaks of a revelation and of the possession of knowledge infinitely joyful, infinitely sad.   It is a face a little frightened, a little proud ; a little timid, a little breaking with joy.   It is the face of a child suddenly become a woman who is also forewarned of future pain yet who must spend herself in her present great joys.   The figure is a masterpiece of the spirit of humanism.   It is as moving and as tender a work as Jan van Eyck's great painting—with which it has something in common—of Arnolfini and his young wife.

The bust of the Madonna that is displayed in the presbytery is of more sophisticated making and more subtle modelling.   Beyond that comparison is profitless, for this too is a masterpiece.   This figure has lost its crown and its left forearm, and the lovely figure of the infant Christ is much mutilated.   Yet what remains conveys the artist's purposes to us as powerfully as if no damage had been done.

The infant Christ is exquisitely placed within the hollow of the right arm so that the figure is at once displayed away from the Mother, yet held (by the placing of the arms and the folds of the robes) within the design of the whole work.   In contrast to the more elaborate modelling of the child's clothes, those of the Madonna are plain and self-effacing.   The artist's purpose was to throw all the weight of attention on the figure of the infant Christ and on the head of the Madonna which leans slightly down towards it.

It is a lovely face ; a face lit by a pride most sweet and human because it lies lightly upon an expression of serene humility.   The exquisitely modelled eyes and lips both speak the simplest of messages : the joy of a mother in her first-born son.   It is only in the withdrawal of the figure from that of the Child that you may catch the whisper of the words : " This also is God."

The third of these fragments of Winchester's medieval masterpieces is the head of the Almighty in the library.   It is small, and is still clearly marked with traces of the colour which once adorned it.   The head is richly crowned and bearded, and is half turned to look far down over the shoulder—as if from the high bridge of Heaven.   The lines of the beard and hair and the embroideries which hang from the crown are carved in bold and flowing curves which enhance the sense of great space beyond the vision of the eyes. The face is of supreme dignity.   The master who created it has wonderfully realized his conception of a Being as old as time, whose age is written deeply on his brow, whose weariness presses heavily upon his eyes, whose authority and sternness have shaped the set of his lips—and yet whose compassion and forbearance informs the whole head with an expression of profound tenderness.

Like the carvings of the Madonna, this fragment is a survival from an age which deeply believed, and yet walked very close with the Family it worshipped.   These were people who had no reason to doubt that the Almighty had created man in his own image.   If that image was divine, it was also human ; moved by the same emotions, the same laughter, the same tears, the same compassion and the same anger as those which the carvers and the artists observed in themselves and saw reflected in the faces of the passers-by in the streets.

There remains, lastly, the headless figure which now stands in the retrochoir and which once, certainly, represented the Synagogue.   This figure of the Synagogue was a common one in early medieval sculpture, and was personified as a woman with bandaged eyes who bore a broken staff.

The question of the correct identification of this figure, however, is irrelevant.   The great distance which separates us from the symbolism of the medieval ages, and the accidents of time that have stripped the statue of all symbolic trappings, have left us now the headless figure of a woman which is one of the glories of Western art ; a masterpiece of such intensity that its meaning is universal and for all time.

The figure is dressed in a flowing robe held at the waist by a girdle which once was of metal and decorated with precious stones.   A cloak hangs over the shoulders and falls in soft folds over the outstretched right arm. The position is one of movement : the right leg presses forward through the veil of robes, the left foot barely touches the ground. The modelling of the robe (so soft and fine that it seems part of the limbs behind it) carries the eye swiftly upward to a point of tension at the right shoulder where the movement is arrested and exquisitely dissolved by the few simple lines of the carving below the throat. The effect, then, is of motion : motion of extraordinary grace and swiftness and lightness. But it is movement composed into a pattern of perfect tranquillity.

Yet the bare outline of the technical details of the figure reveals nothing of its surpassing beauty and of its power to move the heart and mind. It is among the loveliest expressions of feminine grace that have ever been translated in stone : a perpetual ideal of the enchanting beauty of form and movement of which the human body is capable. But it is more than that. The stone not only embodies the warmth and tenderness of a human emotion ; it also transcends it. This statue speaks of the spiritual serenity that all the great religions have sought, and which was the ideal an unknown Christian carver set out to express when he took up his chisel and began to cut away the stone.

II : *Relics of the Kings*

BISHOP HENRY DE BLOIS, politician, castle-builder and faction-leader during the feudal wars of the twelfth century, was also a patron of the arts. To him Winchester Cathedral owes two of its most unusual treasures—the black marble font that stands in the nave, and the collection of the bones of the Saxon kings and their bishops which are now housed in the mortuary chests on the screens of the presbytery.

There are only seven of these lovely and exotic fonts in England, and they are rare in Europe. They were made in the twelfth century near Tournai in Belgium where, on the banks of the River Scheldt, was quarried a hard black marble. For a brief time a flourishing industry was established there which exported a number of square-cut, decorated fonts. Of the seven that reached England, Winchester's is the most elaborately carved and best preserved.

The east and north sides of Winchester's font are decorated with symbolic medallions of the times such as doves picking at vines, and a salamander representing the baptismal fire. The more remarkable panels, however, are those on the west and south which illustrate three legends of the Saint Nicholas of Myra who became a patron saint of children and hence the original of the mundane old gentlemen who preside over the commercialized festivities of our modern Christmas.

On the south the legend is plainly set forth. It shows Saint Nicholas, crozier in hand, presenting a grateful father with a bag of gold while his three daughters and a male figure look happily—even smugly—on. The tale is old and strange and its moral appears at this distance a doubtful one. The father was, we are told, so desperately poor that he decided to sell his three daughters to a brothel. Saint Nicholas, stricken with horror at hearing of this infamous decision, secretly threw a bag of gold into the house by night and continued to do so until the unworthy father was able to catch him at his benevolent work and thank him for it. In addition to the figures of this legend, the panel also shows an almost diagrammatic elevation of a Norman church.

The west panel is more involved, for the incidents of the two legends it illustrates have been much mixed up. The figures in the centre of the panel show first an innkeeper armed with an axe (and behind him his wife) about to strike off the heads of three sleeping boys ; and secondly Saint Nicholas restoring the boys' heads to their bodies after hearing the innkeeper confess that he had chopped the children up because he had run out of meat for his sausages. The figures on the left and right of the panel (and one recumbent figure which has become involved in the scene of the restoration to life of the children) illustrate the tale of a nobleman who, fulfilling a vow made before the birth of a much-desired son, journeyed by sea to Saint Nicholas's church carrying the gift of a gold cup. The child however fell overboard, and left a desolate father to fulfil the vow alone. He offered the cup at the altar, but no sooner had it been placed there than it leaped away. A second and a third time this strange thing happened. And while the nobleman marvelled, his son walked in to the church alive and well.

On the panel, in carvings as naive as is the legend, you may see the family setting out by boat ; the drowned boy floating in the water, gold cup in hand ; and the boy restored to life hand in hand with Saint Nicholas who here faintly smiles as if he were a most proud and happy man.

The story of Winchester's mortuary chests is, however, stranger and more romantic by far than the most extravagant inventions that ever provided a stone-carver with a theme for his chisel. It is strange enough that within them lie the bones of kings who made this island's earliest recorded history and who died more than a thousand years ago. It is stranger still that their sepulchres should be elaborately carved boxes of Italian design which lie ranged upon the top of the screens which enclose the presbytery. It is strangest of all that they have survived the many changes and chances which have visited Winchester since the days of the eclipse of the old Saxon and Danish dynasties.

There are six chests now, and whether the descriptions of the bones that lie in them are accurate no one will ever know. Already in the time of de Blois, who gathered them from the crypt to which they had been transferred from the old Saxon cathedral, and displayed them in leaden sarcophagi, the bones were wonderfully mixed. " Through ignorance as to which were kings and which were bishops," wrote an old chronicler, " there being no inscription on their monuments, the said Bishop Henry placed kings with bishops, and bishops with kings all mixed together." But if the inscriptions on the chests are to be believed, the chests hold all that remains of Cynegils, first Christian King of Wessex (died 643) ; Kenulph, son of Cynegils (died 714) ; Egbert, first " King of all England " (died 836) ; Ethelwulf his son, and father of Alfred the Great (died 858) ; Edmund, Alfred's son (died 946) ; Edred (died 955) ; and Canute (died 1035) whose bones are mingled with those of his wife Emma and of two bishops, Wina and Alwyn. This last chest also claims to contain the bones of Rufus, but as we have seen, Rufus most probably lies beneath the stone in the centre of the choir.

These illustrious bones must once have rested on the walls of the old Norman choir, for it was surely only the tradition of their display in this part of the church which caused Bishop Fox to replace them in a similar position on his fine new screens. Accordingly, Fox had eight magnificent chests made in a style suitable to the Renaissance modelling of his screens, and transferred the relics to them—when the bones, already mixed enough, were further mingled together.

The eight chests were still there when John Evelyn visited Winchester in 1642 and wrote in his diary : " I visited the Castle, Schole, Church and King Arthur's Round Table, but specially the Church and its Saxon Kings' monuments, which I esteemed a worthy antiquity."

A few months later these " worthy antiquities " suffered the strangest translation of their strange history. The Roundhead soldiers, perhaps understandably outraged by relics that seemed to sanctify the institution of monarchy, hurled down several of the chests and threw the bones about the floor of the choir. Some they picked up to throw at stained glass windows that were beyond the reach of the butts of their pikes. When Evelyn visited Winchester again in 1685 he wrote in his diary : " There are still the coffins of the six Saxon Kings, whose bones had been scatter'd by the Sacrilegious Rebells of 1642, in expectation, I suppose, of finding some valuable reliques, and afterwards gathered up againe and put into new chestes, which stand above the stalls of the Quire."

The soldiers had destroyed four of Fox's chests. What remained of the bones were placed in two chests, made after the Restoration, in the same pattern as the old. The bones have been examined two or three times since then, but (except that in recent years the two remaining fifteenth-century inner chests, with their still brilliant decorations, have been removed and may be seen in the north aisle of the retrochoir) the relics have remained at last in peace after much wandering. Some at least of them are those of the ancient kings who were the makers of England, and who first dedicated the ground over which they lie to the worship of the Christian faith. Their sepulchres are a profoundly moving symbol of the tenacious survival through great changes—even through great disasters—of the English folk and their old and not inglorious story.

12 : " Lasting Mansions "

FEW visitors to Winchester can miss seeing the tombstone of Thomas Thetcher, one time a grenadier in the North Hants Militia. It is one of those curiosities which might have been invented to cheer the often laborious minds of the compilers of guide books and the writers of cathedral histories. It is true that it is a little indecorous. Many people no doubt agree with Canon John Vaughan who condemned it, in 1919, as having an " unseemly inscription " and of appeal only to "uncultured visitors". Thomas Thetcher's memorial remains in the Cathedral yard, however, to affront a cultured sensibility with its reminder that there are many gates by which mortal man may enter the mansions of Death. For this militiaman died on May 12, 1764, at the age of twenty-six " of a violent Fever contracted by drinking Small Beer when hot ".

His regimental comrades could not forbear to draw a moral or two. They carved on Thomas Thetcher's tombstone :

> Here sleeps in peace a Hampshire Grenadier,
> Who caught his death by drinking cold small Beer,
> Soldiers be wise from his untimely fall
> And when ye're hot drink Strong or none at all.

To this they later added the lines :

> An honest Soldier never is forgot,
> Whether he die by Musket or by Pot.

Whatever else these prankish lines illustrate they are a reminder that the living, confronted with the knowledge of the inescapable exit that awaits them all, simply cannot help moralizing about it : especially when they carve a tombstone or merely come to look upon the memorials of the dead. Even Horace Walpole, least sententious of men, was unable to resist the common habit. It was after a visit to Winchester that he wrote to Richard Bentley : " How much power and ambition under half a dozen stones ! I own I grow to look on tombs as lasting mansions instead of observing them for curious architecture ".

Like all our cathedrals, Winchester has provided hundreds of English folk with their lasting mansions or memorials. They are all there : the sinners and the saints, the notable and the humble, tradesmen and bishops, authors and soldiers, prebendaries and their families, noblemen and their descendants. The bones of kings mighty in their day, and the remains of Thomas Thetcher, Hampshire militiaman, have made a common journey to ground which has been sacred to the English dead for years beyond the counting.

Like signposts passed upon a long journey, the Cathedral remembrances of the dead make a record of the English progress. From the conversion of Wessex to Christianity in the seventh century to the present day, not a century has failed to leave some memorial record of its struggles, its beliefs, its fears, its ideals or its tastes. All of the vigorous drive of the Victorians for colonial expansion and of their dismal tastes in decoration are recorded in the many military memorials to men who fell at Salamanca, Sevastopol and Delhi; or in Burma, the Sudan, Afghanistan, South Africa and many another place far from home. The reticent good-breeding and decorum of eighteenth-century provincial society is preserved for us in the memorials to the many Eyres who claimed the Venerable Chapel for their own and displayed their family arms (*argent on a chevron sable, three quatrefoils or*) upon the dignified iron gate which enclosed the privacy of their dead. The worldly pomp of the medieval bishops and the dread with which they often parted with the living are told in the splendid chapels they built to cover their bones.

But it is the individual tombs and memorials which we seek out or best remember. William the Conqueror's young son Richard, Duke of Beorn, lies buried here, killed as his uncle was by an arrow while hunting in the forest. Peter de Rupibus—financier, engineer, general of armies, civil servant, crusader and (finally) Bishop of Winchester from 1204 to 1238—is commemorated by the oldest effigy in the Cathedral. Not far away from him is the fine figure of Sir Arnald de Gaveston who professed himself—at about the same period as de Rupibus—only a soldier, and whose shield hangs at the ready on his left arm while his right lies vigilantly on the handle of his sword. Behind both these tombs, on the east wall of the retrochoir is the lovely medieval wall-tablet of Audemar, Bishop of Winchester 1250-60, whose cupped hands hold his heart—which was all of Audemar that was buried in this place. He never was in Winchester. Indeed he was made priest only in the year of his death and ten years after his election to the see of Winchester. He died in Paris where his body lies. His heart, he asked, should be carried to the Cathedral whose revenues he had drawn but which he had never served.

Another bishop seldom seen at Winchester was Peter Mews who died in 1706. After his death a petition was presented to Queen Anne praying for a more active bishop inasmuch as " the late bishop was entirely careless of discharging the duty of his function so that we have suffered under all the inconveniences of neglected visitation and want of confirmations." Peter Mews was a Royalist and a man of action. He had been many times wounded in the Civil War, which did not discourage him from hurrying out of Winchester (he was nearly seventy) when he heard of Monmouth's landing in the west, to busy himself with the King's artillery and receive yet another severe wound at the battle of Sedgemoor. His memorial in the Chapel of the Guardian Angels is appropriately decorated with military symbols, but the appearance of the mitre and crozier among them is perhaps not so fitting.

A sweeter memorial of this period is the stone above the grave of Izaak Walton. Walton is not the only author whose stone is a place of pilgrimage in Winchester Cathedral. In the north aisle of the nave Jane Austen was buried on July 18, 1817 shortly after she had moved to Winchester during her last illness. Perhaps lovers of Jane Austen will hardly recognize her from the inscription carved on her grave.

" In memory of Jane Austen, youngest daughter of the late Revd. George Austen formerly Rector of Steventon in this County. She departed this life on the 15th of July 1817 aged 41 after a long illness supported with the patience and the hopes of a Christian. The benevolence of her heart the sweetness of her temper and the extraordinary endowments of her mind obtained the regard of all who knew her and the warmest love of her intimate connections. Their grief is in proportion to their affection, they know their loss to be irreparable, but in their deepest affliction they are consoled by a firm though humble hope that her charity, devotion, faith and purity have rendered her soul acceptable in the sight of her Redeemer ".

It is a remarkable inscription. If ever a time came in which readers of novels forgot

Jane Austen, nothing in the stiff epitaph would lead them to suppose that it covered the remains of a writer who was once loved as authors are rarely loved. Jane Austen, whose genius was for the observation of life's little ironies, would have appreciated it.

Jane Austen's body was among the last to be laid to rest within the Cathedral walls. Since the middle of the nineteenth century only monuments and tablets to the dead have been installed to continue the record of the lives of men and women who have worshipped in the Cathedral.

How various and how noble the record is the stones of the Cathedral show. It is a record also exquisitely summarized in a work which still proceeds and which has given Winchester its most modern treasures. These are the series of embroideries which decorate the cushions of the choir stalls and which are the work of the society of Winchester Cathedral Broderers. The devoted patience and skill which has gone to the making of these lovely pieces of craftsmanship is in the ancient medieval tradition when time was not measured only by the money-standard nor a labour subject to the accountancy of profit and loss. A series of medallions worked in rich colours sets out the Winchester story. It begins with the symbol of the Tree of Life as a memorial to the pre-Christian worship at the sacred springs on the banks of the Itchen river. It ends with the badges of the regiments of the British Army which have for many years been based in Winchester and whose memorials and banners are to be found in the nave of the Cathedral, and with a medallion which tells of the years from 1905-12 when the east aisle and the south side of the nave were restored and saved from the great peril of complete collapse.

It is an appropriate symbol of our time. In this century the great Cathedral church has been devotedly saved from the ruin of time and threats of total war, and has been much freed from the ravages of the restorers. The House that was bequeathed us by the Age of Faith has been preserved. It will pass to our descendants with the signs that, in an age perplexed and restless and yet tenacious in the face of disaster, there were among us some who were undismayed by the threats to those values which have thus far shaped our destinies and of which Winchester Cathedral is one of the most precious embodiments that we possess.

Part of a page from the twelfth-century Winchester Bible in the Cathedral Library.
The drawing is an illustration to the first book of Maccabees.

LIST OF ILLUSTRATIONS

LIST OF ILLUSTRATIONS (contd.)

The approach to the Cathedral from the north-west corner of the close is made through an avenue of ancient lime trees.

The entrance to the Deanery in the close. Around the triple arch, of thirteenth-century workmanship, pilgrims once gathered to receive doles of bread and pence.

43

The great size of the Cathedral may best be appreciated looking to the north from the roof of Winchester College Chapel (above). The lower picture shows a nearer view of the choir and south transept.

44

Looking down on the east end of the Cathedral from St. Giles Hill which rises to the north of the road from London. The hill was the site of Winchester's great annual fair in medieval times.

45

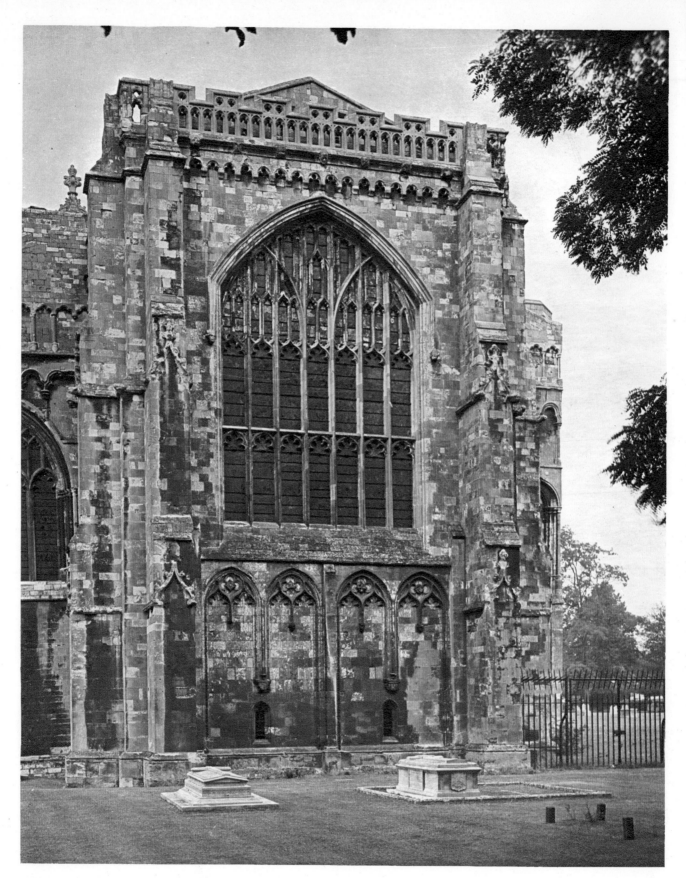

When the infant son of Henry VII was baptized in the Cathedral in 1486, his mother made a gift of money to the Prior. With this money, the Lady Chapel was extended to the east.

The glorious flying buttresses which support the walls and roof of the choir were the work of Bishop Richard Fox,
1500-28.   His device of a pelican can be seen carved at the heads of two of the buttresses.

47

The tower and choir from the north-east. The choir was reconstructed in the sixteenth century and the richness of its decoration is in striking contrast to the simplicity of the work of the four previous centuries.

48

The north transept has not greatly altered since it was built by the Norman bishops.   A sixteenth-century builder
pierced the gable with a rose-window which illuminates nothing but roof timbers.

Few visitors know that even the severe façade of the west front is enriched with imps and gargoyles, devils and portrait heads. The figure of a bishop is that of William of Wykeham, the Cathedral's greatest benefactor.

The west front is not among the Cathedral's architectural glories : its design lacks proportion.   It was erected in the middle of the fourteenth century in place of the great turreted porch of the Norman builders.

Winchester's nave is among the most precious legacies England has of the work of the Gothic builders.   The work was begun about the year 1350 and was largely inspired by Wykeham, greatest of the Bishops of Winchester.

The nave, looking west. The great piers and arches were re-fashioned, bay by bay, from the three-storeyed Norman nave. On the extreme left is part of the chantry of Edington, who built the great west window.

The Gothic builders crowned their buildings with glorious and massive vaults without benefit of text-books and formulæ.   At Winchester, moreover, they were artists of genius.

54

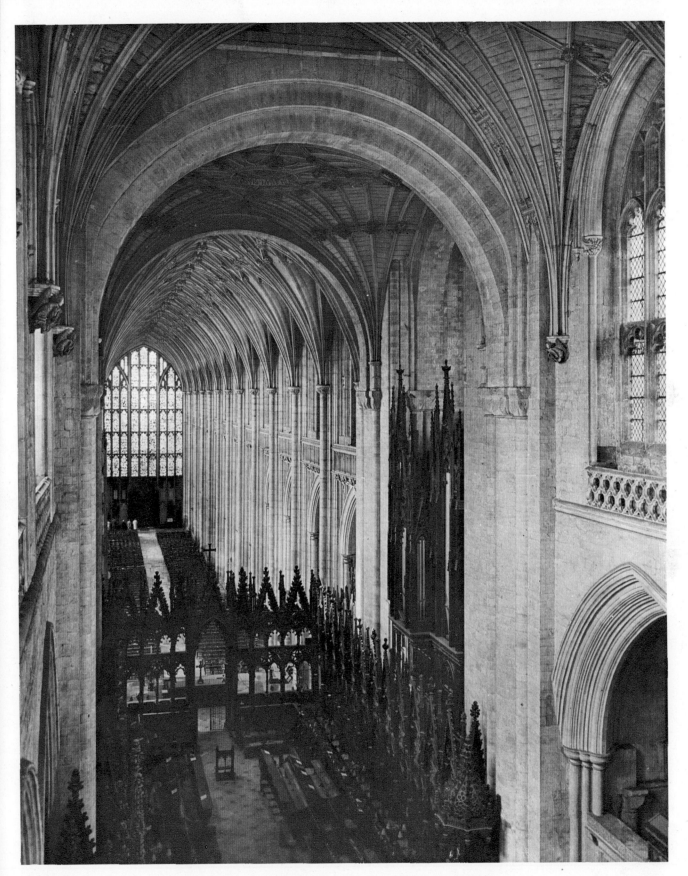

From the top of the reredos there is this magnificent view of the nave framed by the enormous arch which is one of the four which the Normans built to support the weight of the tower.

These bronze statues of James I and Charles I are the work of Hubert le Sueur. They were buried in a garden during the Commonwealth and restored to the Cathedral when Charles II became King.

The statues of the Stuart kings stand on either side of the west door above which hang the colours of the Royal Hampshire Regiment, for long associated with the city of Winchester.

This view across the nave dais shows—on the nearer faces of the two right-hand piers—the original pillars and capitals which, in Norman times, supported the arches of the lowest storey of the nave.

A broad flight of steps leads from the south transept to the retrochoir. Beyond the old Norman arch are the choir screens which were among the last of the pre-Reformation additions to the fabric of the Cathedral.

The iron gates have divided the south transept from the aisles of the retrochoir for upwards of eight centuries. They are probably the oldest—certainly they are among the most beautiful—of their kind in England.

60

The view of the south aisle of the nave across the south transept. In the foreground the original Norman arch remains. Beyond it are the arches as they were re-fashioned by Wykeham's craftsmen.

Jane Austen's tomb in the north aisle of the nave.   The inscription gives no indication that Jane Austen was one of the greatest of English writers, or that she had ever written a book.

The balconies which run the length of the nave below the clerestory are enriched with many fine bosses.   Among them are busts of angels, portrait heads, heraldic devices and foliages.

The twelfth-century font of black Tournai stone. On the west and south sides (above) are carved legends of the life of Saint Nicholas. Below : detail of the carving on the south panel. (See text, page 35.)

Above: two of the superb initial letters from the twelfth-century Winchester Bible which is preserved in the Cathedral library. Below: part of an uncompleted page from the Bible. It is the drawing of a master hand.

Behind the soaring screen of this chantry lies the tomb of William of Wykeham. In this place Wykeham stood as a poor boy watching the rituals of the monks—and perhaps dreaming of his future greatness.

Like patterned lace hung high upon the poles of a tent the roof of Wykeham's chantry provides a princely canopy for the sleeping figure of the great Bishop.

The effigy of William of Wykeham.   At his head two angels fiercely guard his pillow.   At his feet are, it is thought, the figures of the three master-craftsmen to whose genius we owe the glories of the nave.

The chantry of Bishop Edington in the nave. It is the earliest and simplest of the chantries. Within it lies the fine alabaster effigy of the man who began the reconstruction of the nave.

The transepts remain much as they were when the Normans built them shortly after the Conquest. This view of the clerestory and triforium of the south transept shows the massive scale on which the Normans worked.

The north transept. The entire Cathedral was once built to the imposing and simple plan that is preserved in this part of the structure. It is the work of a conquering race.

71

The Venerable Chapel in the south transept, with its superb Gothic stone screen and delicate eighteenth-century ironwork. The original purpose served by this chapel has long been forgotten.

Prior Silkstede's Chapel occupies the bay next to the Venerable Chapel.   The Prior's Christian name—Thomas—is carved on the shields which decorate the cornice.

Above : The Chapel of the Holy Sepulchre in the north transept, once one of the holiest of the Cathedral's holy places. Below : the library which was the gift, in the seventeenth century, of Bishop Morley.

74

The superb remnants of the early thirteenth-century wall paintings which once enriched the walls of the Chapel of
the Holy Sepulchre.   Beneath the head of Christ is a Deposition from the Cross.

The west face of the choir screen is a nineteenth-century structure in the style of the choir stalls behind it.   It is doubtful whether it is the best solution to the problem of separating the choir from the nave.

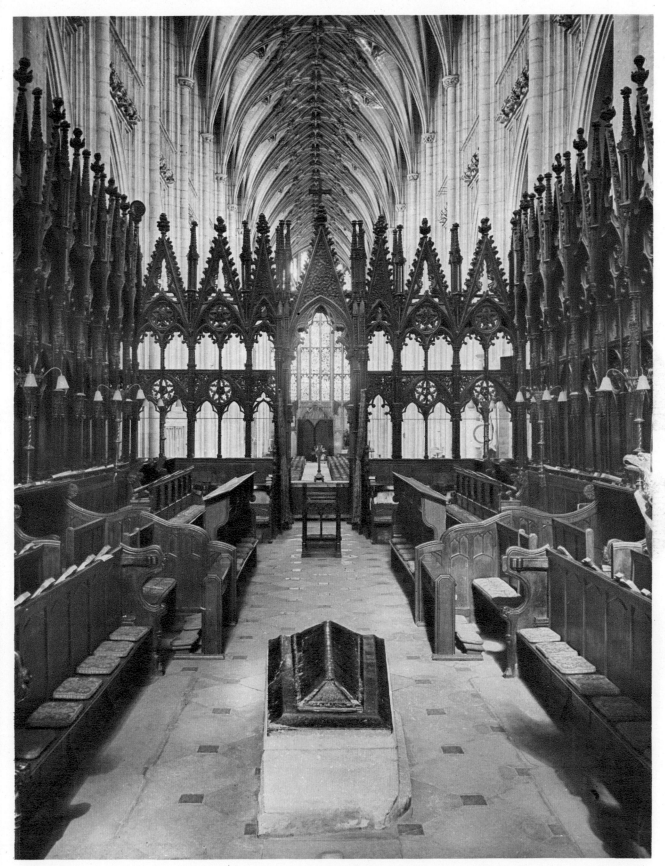

The choir.   In the foreground is an unnamed tomb which is believed to be that of William Rufus who was buried in the Cathedral (" with the grief of few ") in the year 1100.

Detail of one of the canopies in the choir stalls.   Although the elements of the design are simple, the decoration is exuberant.   Each of the points of the cusps is, for instance, carved with foliage or a portrait head.

78

The choir stalls were begun in 1308 and completed seven years later. They are the oldest and loveliest wooden stalls that any English cathedral possesses.

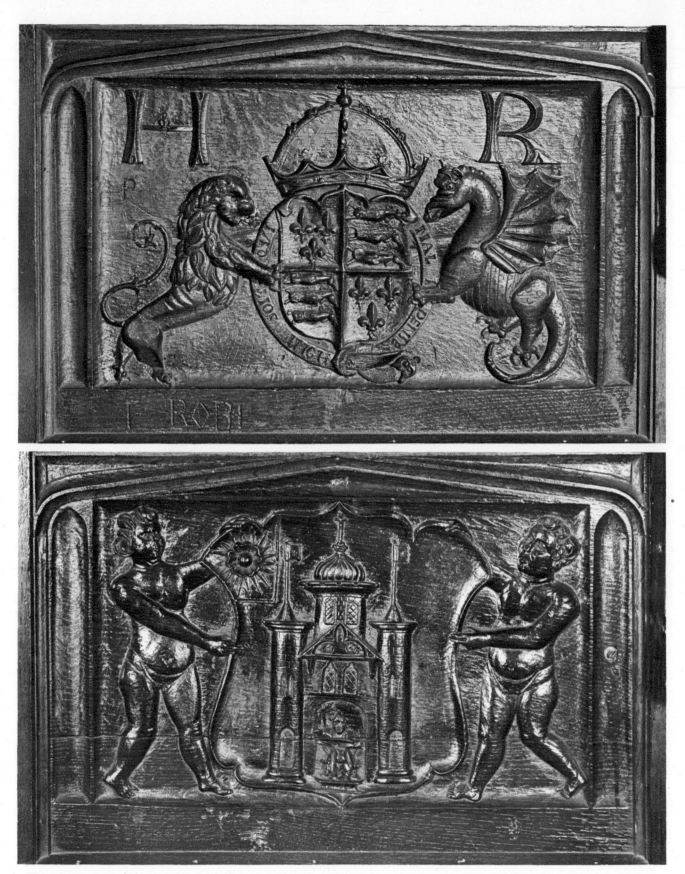

The sixteenth-century panels which decorate the sub-stalls of the choir were carved by Italian craftsmen. Above: Henry VIII's coat of arms. Below: the arms granted to the Dean and Chapter by the College of Heralds.

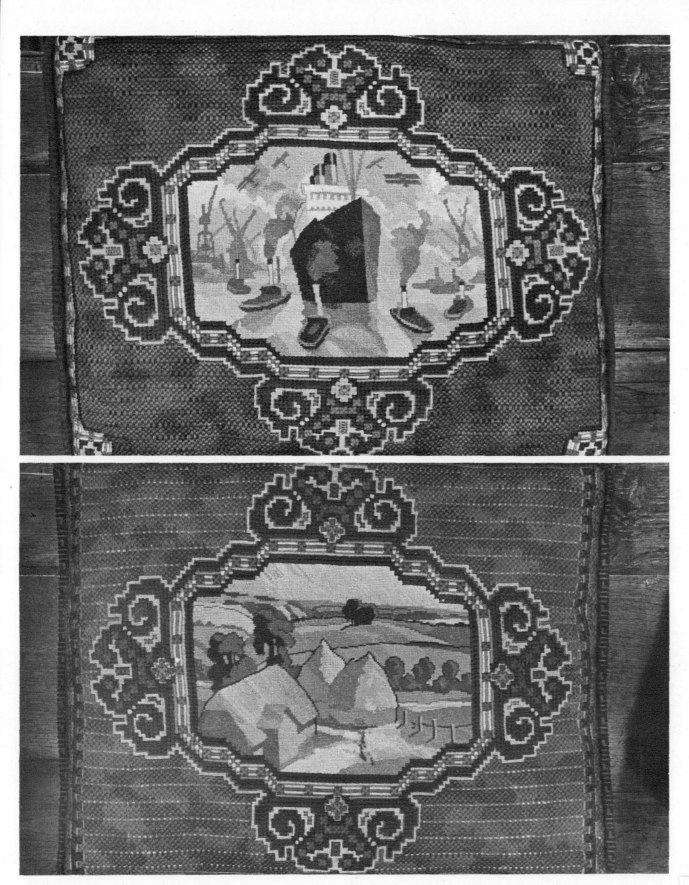

Two examples of the lovely modern work of the Winchester Broderers whose cushions enrich the choir stalls.   These
embroidered medallions show the liner *Queen Mary* in Southampton Water and a typical Hampshire scene.

Carved misericords in the choir stalls.   The carvings are all full of life, of observation of simple, homely things, and
of the freakish or impish fancies of the medieval craftsmen.

82

This splendid pulpit was placed in the choir by Prior Silkstede shortly before the Reformation. It is enriched with a design in the form of skeins of silk—a punning reference to the donor's name.

The tower was roofed with a wooden vault in 1635. In the centre is an ingenious Latin inscription whose larger letters may be arranged to spell the date of the vault's construction.

The ringing chamber. The first Norman tower collapsed in 1107. Comparison with the work illustrated on page 70 shows the technical progress a new generation of builders had made.

Details of some of the wooden bosses on the roof of the presbytery.   Left :   arms of the Saxon and Danish kings.
Right :   arms of Henry VII, an emblem of his victory at Bosworth Field, and arms of Bishop Richard Fox.

Part of the presbytery roof with its unique collection of Passion emblems.   Among them can be seen the three dice, the crowing cock, a Veronica, heads of the High Priests, and the cup of vinegar.

The stone screens were built to enclose the presbytery by Bishop Fox.   When they were completed, the bones of the
ancient Saxon kings were placed in mortuary chests upon the cornice.

88

Above : this mortuary chest is said to contain the relics of Canute, Rufus, Queen Emma and two Saxon bishops, Wini and Alwyn. Below : the ancient inner shell of one of the mortuary chests.

89

The presbytery, reredos and high altar. Here, the devotion and genius of many generations of English artists and craftsmen have created an enclosure of surpassing beauty.

The reredos.   So perfect is its design and ornamentation that the great mass of stone appears to hang between the walls as lightly as though it were a curtain of lace.

91

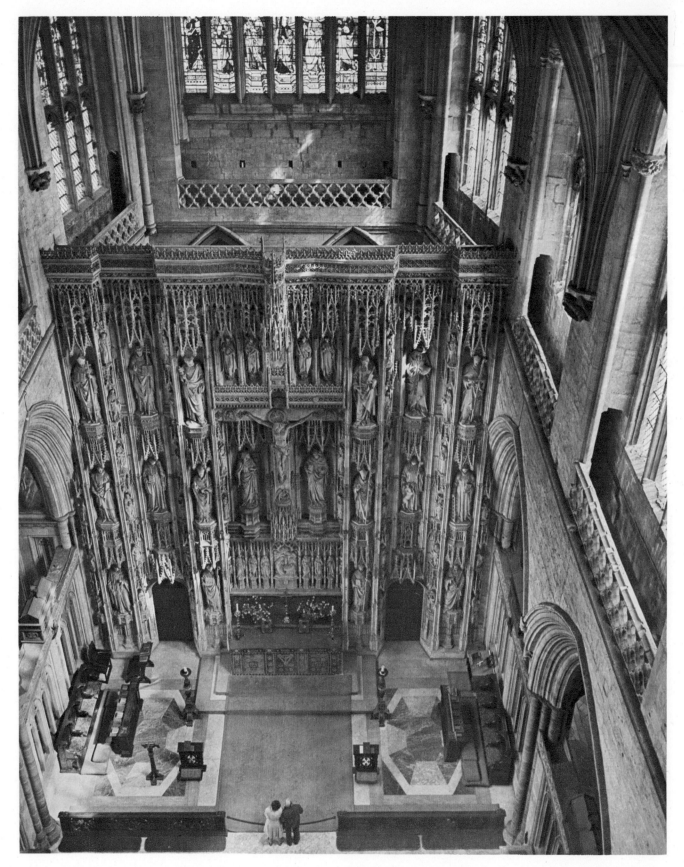

The high altar and reredos seen from the bell-chamber. Behind the stone screen is the enclosure of the feretory where once were housed the relics of the saints.

A detailed view of the canopy of the reredos reveals the exquisite refinement of the carving.   The stone figures are
modern replacements of those destroyed at the Reformation.

93

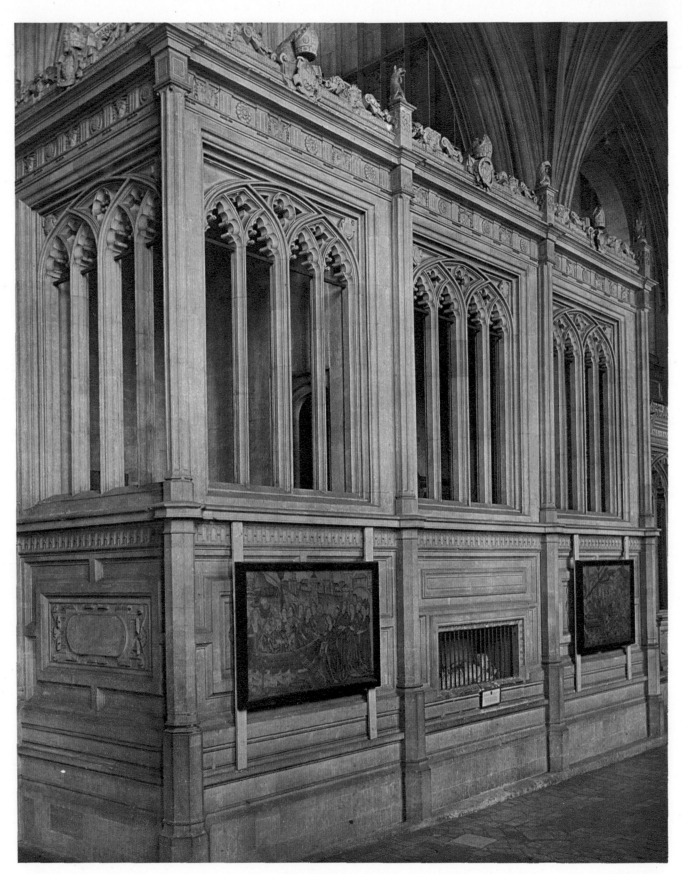

The chantry of Stephen Gardiner in the north aisle of the retrochoir. It is the last monument of the Old Faith in the Cathedral, and is of indifferent workmanship and mixed styles.

94

A number of extremely rich canopies decorate the rear wall of the feretory.   The empty pedestals once held figures
of the old Saxon kings and bishops.

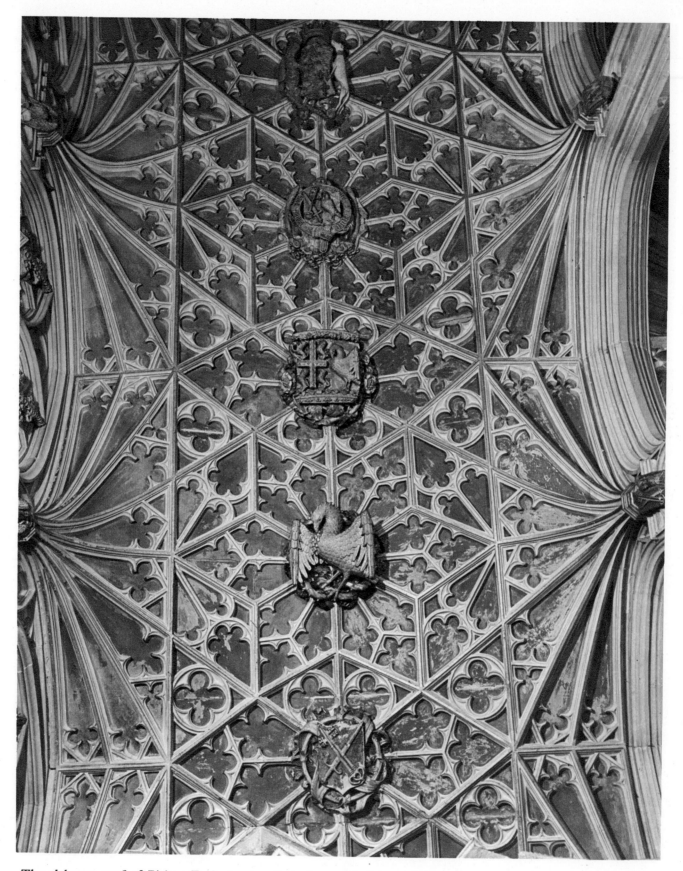

The elaborate roof of Bishop Fox's chantry. It is decorated with coats of arms, most of them of Fox or of his bishoprics. His device of a pelican is prominently displayed.

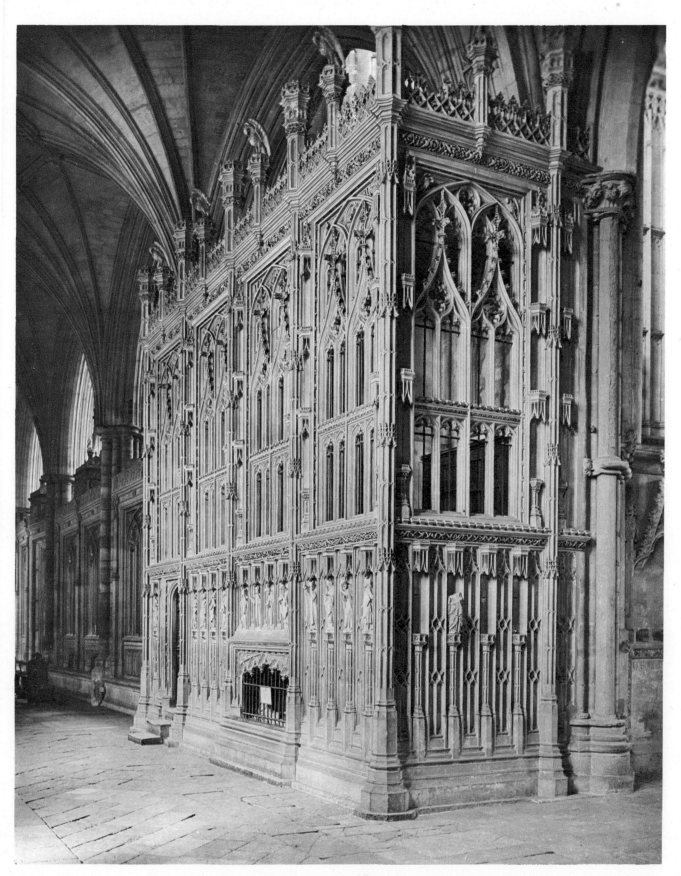

Fox's chantry in the south aisle of the retrochoir. It is perhaps the most lovely of the chantries. For all the elaboration of its detail, the effect is one of elegance and simplicity.

The south aisle of the retrochoir. The ancient timber foundations rotted away beneath this corner of the Cathedral, and the walls, though restored, now lean at unexpected angles.

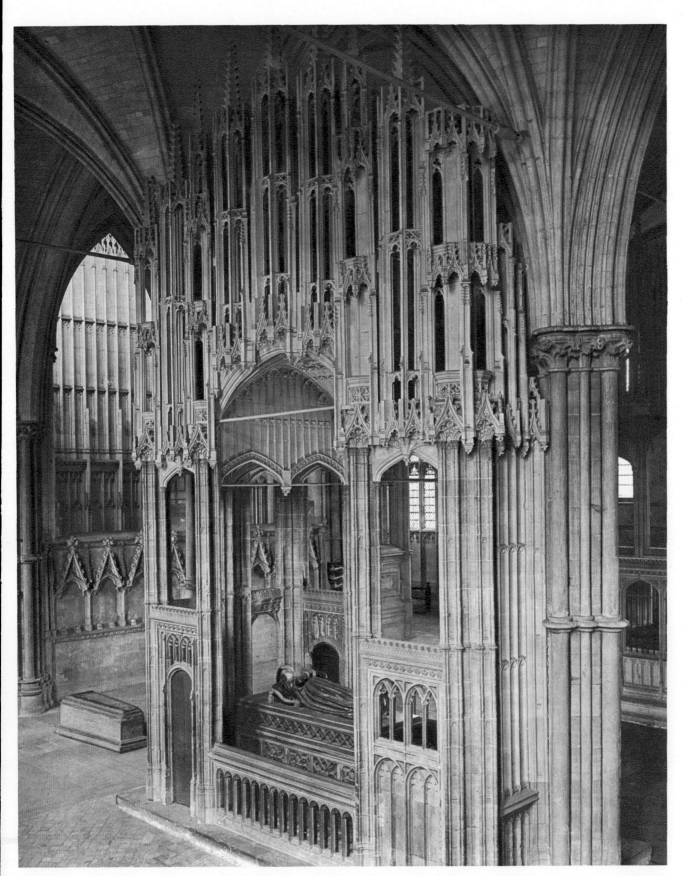

The Purbeck marble chantry of Cardinal Beaufort, Bishop of Winchester, 1404-47.   It is a housing for the lying-in-state of a prince rather than a place for withdrawal and for prayer.

99

The superb stone canopy above the effigy of Bishop Wayneflete. The angel displays the Bishop's arms which are also those of Wayneflete's foundation of Magdalen College, Oxford.

Bishop Wayneflete's chantry in the retrochoir. It is built of dazzling white stone to the same majestic design of arched screens supporting a pinnacled canopy as that of Cardinal Beaufort.

The roof of the Chapel of the Guardian Angels is gloriously painted with medallions of angels and a pattern of foliage and azure stars.   The work is of the thirteenth century.

The Chapel of the Guardian Angels in the north-east corner of the Cathedral. The graceful Early English arcading and pier shafts were built by Bishop de Lucy, 1188-1204.

Four of the twenty-two late fifteenth-century wall paintings in the Lady Chapel. The originals (many seriously faded) are concealed behind these carefully executed copies. All of them illustrate legends of Our Lady.

The Lady Chapel consists of two halves. The nearer half is of Early English workmanship. At the end of the fifteenth century it was extended eastward as the result of a gift of money by Elizabeth, wife of Henry VII.

The noble roof of the Lady Chapel is enriched with bosses of the royal house of Tudor and of Winchester prelates, and with a superb medallion in the centre of the Almighty enthroned in judgement.

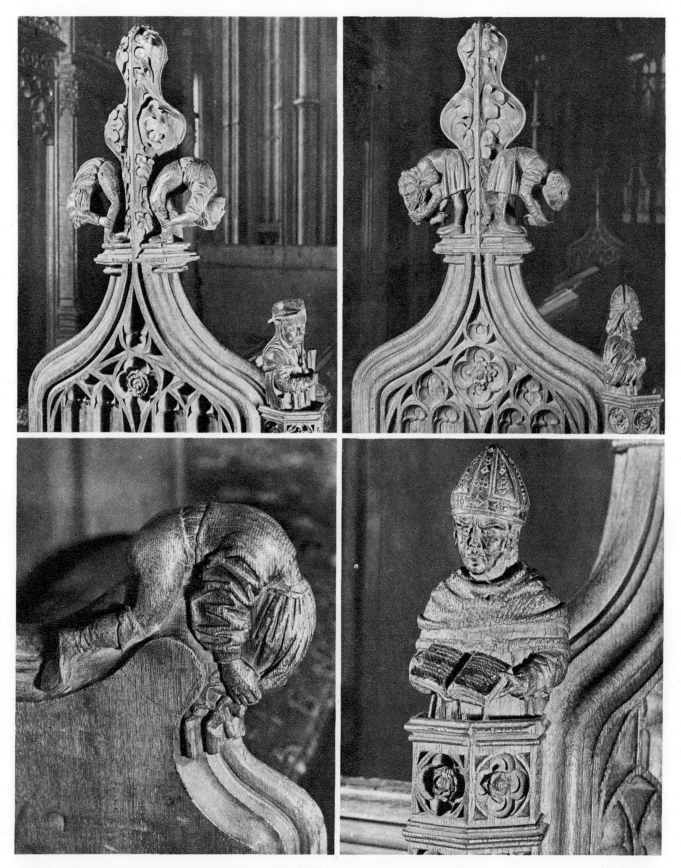

Details of some of the woodcarving in the stalls of the Lady Chapel. Above left: a pair of dancing tumblers; above right: two beggars. Below left: a choir-boy with his head caught in his surplice; below right: a bishop.

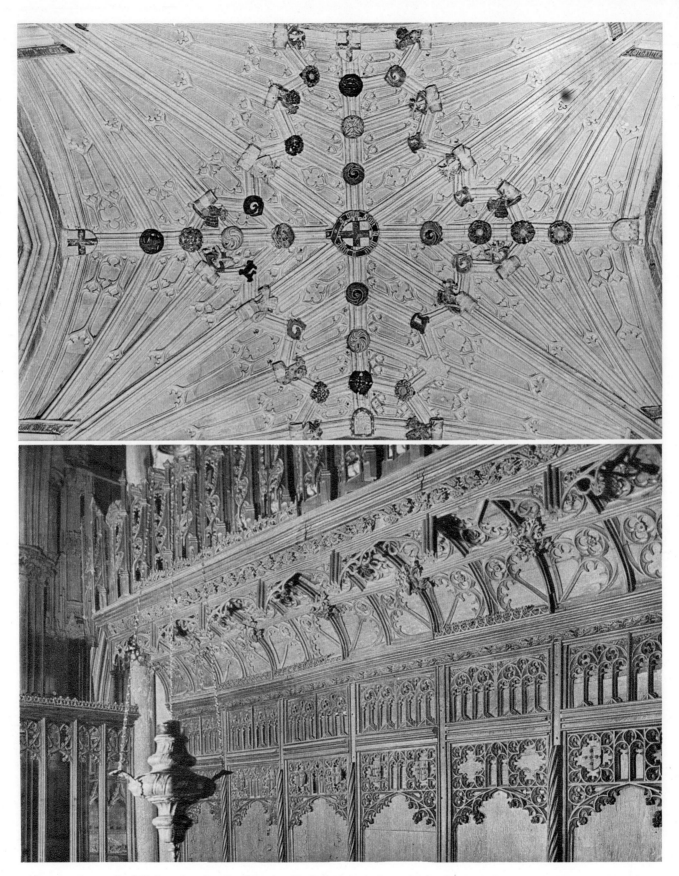

Above : the roof of Bishop Langton's Chapel. Its bosses include a series of punning representations of the names of the Bishop and his Prior, Hunton. Below : the rich woodwork of the chapel's stalls.

Langton's Chapel in the south-east corner of the Cathedral.   It was enclosed by magnificent carved wood screens as the chantry of the Bishop, who died in 1500.

The breaking of the stone sculpture of our cathedrals during the Reformation was a loss too great to be measured. We can appreciate the nature of the loss by studying this fragment of a Madonna now in the presbytery.

This broken head of the Almighty in the Cathedral library escaped complete destruction by the hammers of the iconoclasts. Can ever the phrase " the Ancient of Days " have been more perfectly expressed in stone?

A fragment of a Madonna which now stands in the triforium of the south transept.   The unknown artist created an
exquisite image of the young Mother.   It is a triumph of the humanistic spirit.

This medieval figure of a woman (probably symbolic of the Synagogue) now stands in the retrochoir. One of the most precious of Winchester's treasures, it is also one of the glories of Western sculpture.

A GLOSSARY OF ARCHITECTURAL AND ECCLESIASTICAL TERMS

Abacus : The slab constituting the top member of a capital.

Ambulatory : A walk ; especially the aisle enclosing an apse.

Apse : A semi-circular recess.

Arabesque: An intertwined style of ornamentation.

Arcade : A series of arches.

Ashlar : Stonework of a regular, square shape.

Aumbry : A receptacle for alms ; a small niche with a door.

Ball-flower : A stone or wood enrichment, common in fourteenth-century architecture.

Bay : A section of wall between buttresses ; a wall recess or arched opening.

Benedictional : A prayer-book.

Boss : A prominence, knob or stud ; an ornamental protuberance of a ceiling.

Buttress : Stonework built against a wall to strengthen it.

Capital : The upper section of a pillar.

Chancel : The east part of a church containing the altar.

Chantry : A chapel endowed for the daily celebration of mass for the soul of one deceased.

Cinquefoil : An ornamentation resembling five leaves.

Clerestory : The windowed upper part of a church above the roofs of the aisles.

Consistory court : An ecclesiastical court or assembly.

Corbel : A projection from a wall, generally of stone.

Crocket : An ornamentation placed at intervals on the sides of a gable.

Cusp : A projecting curve ; especially in tracery.

Drip-stone : The outer moulding of an arch. (Also label.)

Enrichment : Recurring ornamentation on a moulding.

Feretory : A repository for shrines.

Finial : An ornamentation at the top of a gable, pinnacle, and the like.

Flying buttress : An open-arched support built from pier to wall.

Foliate : To ornament with leaf-like carvings.

Groin : The angle at the intersection of roof vaultings.

Justiciar : One who dispenses the law.

Label : The outer moulding of an arch. (Also drip-stone.)

Lancet : An Early English window with a pointed head.

Lectionary : A mass-book containing the epistles and gospels to be read at services.

Lierne : One of a number of short ribs supporting the vault and knitting the main arch-ribs together, which in turn transfer the weight to the shafts beneath.

Misericord or *Miserere :* A seat in a choir stall, hinged, often with carvings on the underside.

Moulding : A projecting line of stone.

Nave : The body of a church (from the west front to the chancel).

Ogee : (Of an arch.) A compound arch shaped somewhat like the letter S—that is, with a concave and a convex curve.

Pier : A supporting pillar ; a wall section between windows.

Pilaster : A pillar set partly in a wall.

Piscina : A receptacle set in a niche at the side of an altar to receive the water used during a service.

Prebendary : An ecclesiastic holding the living of a canon.

Pulpitum : A stone screen dividing monastic cathedrals into two parts : the east, for the rituals of the Order ; the west, for public services and the devotions of pilgrims.

Purbeck marble : A blue, grey or greenish limestone from the stone strata which runs from Purbeck in Dorset to the Yorkshire coast.

Quatrefoil : An ornamentation resembling four leaves.

Rebus : An enigmatic illustration of a name, suggesting its syllables.

Reredos : An ornamental screen set behind and above an altar.

Retrochoir : That part of a church to the rear of the high altar.

Return stalls : Stalls in the chancel facing the high altar.

Roodloft : A gallery above the carved screen dividing nave and choir.

Shaft : That part of a pillar between base and capital.

Spandrel : The surface enclosed by the outer curve of an arch and its surrounding framework.

String course : A horizontal line of mouldings in a wall.

Suffragan : An assistant bishop of a diocese.

Transept : The transverse arms of a cruciform church.

Trefoil : An ornamentation resembling three leaves.

Triforium : The gallery above the aisles.

Tympanum : The surface over a doorway or window enclosed by the lintel and a surmounting arch.

Undercroft : A vault.

Voussoir : One of the stones or bricks of which an arch is formed.

A plan of WINCHESTER CATHEDRAL

West Front

Nave

Dais

Izaak Walton, from the stained glass window in Silkstede's Chapel

KEY

1. THE BISHOP'S CONSISTORY COURT
2. BOOK OF REMEMBRANCE : THE ROYAL HAMPSHIRE REGIMENT
3. BOOK OF REMEMBRANCE : THE RIFLE BRIGADE
4. BOOK OF REMEMBRANCE : THE KING'S ROYAL RIFLE CORPS
5. JANE AUSTEN'S TOMB
6. CHANTRY OF WILLIAM OF WYKEHAM
7. ANCIENT NORMAN FONT
8. CHANTRY OF BISHOP EDINGTON
9. FORMER TREASURY OF BISHOP DE BLOIS